I've been gathering and reading a bunch of reference materials to do this pirate story. However, the pirates that I admired so much in my youth hardly ever left written records of their history. I guess they were just too busy having fun on their adventures that they forgot to leave their stories for future generations. That's just the trouble with those darned pirates.

–*Eiichiro Oda, 1997*

· AUTHOR BIOGRAPHY ·

Eiichiro Oda began his manga career in 1992 at the age of 17, when his one-shot cowboy manga *Wanted!* won second place in the coveted Tezuka manga awards. Oda went on to work as an assistant to some of the biggest manga artists in the industry, including Nobuhiro Watsuki, before winning the Hop Step Award for new manga artists. His pirate adventure *One Piece*, which debuted in *Weekly Shonen Jump* magazine in 1997, quickly became one of the most popular manga in Japan.

EAST BLUE
ONE PIECE

ONE PIECE: EAST BLUE 1-2-3

SHONEN JUMP Manga Omnibus Edition
A compilation of the graphic novel volumes 1–3

STORY & ART BY EIICHIRO ODA

English Adaptation: Lance Caselman
Translation: Andy Nakatani
Touch-up Art & Lettering: Bill Schuch (volumes 1–2), Bill Schuch & Walden Wang (volume 3)
Design: Frances Liddell (Omnibus edition cover), Sean Lee (graphic novel volumes 1–3)
Editor: Jason Thompson (volume 1), Shaenon K. Garrity (volume 2), Megan Bates & Shaenon K. Garrity (volume 3)

Printed in the U.S.A.

Published by VIZ Media, LLC
P.O. Box 77010
San Francisco, CA 94107

11
Omnibus edition first printing, December 2009
Eleventh printing, May 2018

RATED
T
FOR
TEEN
PARENTAL ADVISORY
ONE PIECE is rated T for Teen and is recommended for ages 13 and up. This volume contains fantasy violence and tobacco usage.
ratings.viz.com

viz
media

SHONEN
JUMP

www.viz.com

www.shonenjump.com

ONE PIECE
ONE PIECE

Vol. 1
ROMANCE DAWN

STORY AND ART BY
EIICHIRO ODA

ONE PIECE
ONE PIECE

Vol. 1
ROMANCE DAWN

CONTENTS

ONE PIECE
ONE PIECE

CHAPTER 1: ROMANCE DAWN

GOLD ROGER, THE "KING OF THE PIRATES," HAD ACHIEVED IT ALL.
WEALTH, FAME AND POWER HAD ALL BEEN HIS.

NOT SURPRISINGLY, THE FINAL WORDS HE SPOKE BEFORE THEY LOPPED OFF HIS HEAD INSPIRED ADVENTURERS THROUGHOUT THE WORLD TO SAIL THE SEAS.

MY TREASURE? WHY, IT'S RIGHT WHERE I LEFT IT...
SMIRK
IT'S YOURS IF YOU CAN FIND IT... BUT YOU'LL HAVE TO SEARCH THE **WHOLE WORLD**!

THE WORLD...

RROAR

SHUNK!

...IS ABOUT TO WITNESS *A GREAT ERA OF* **PIRACY!**

CHAPTER 1
ロマンス　ドーン
ROMANCE DAWN
—THE DAWN OF ADVENTURE—

A SMALL HARBOR VILLAGE

ONE YEAR AGO...
...A PIRATE SHIP MADE THE VILLAGE ITS BASE.

FWAP
THE WIND BLOWS FROM THE EAST.
HEY, LUFFY! WHAT'RE YOU UP TO NOW?!
HMPH!
AND THE VILLAGE IS AT PEACE.

I'VE HAD IT WITH YOU GUYS!! NOW YOU'LL HAVE TO TAKE ME SERIOUSLY!!

ARRGH!

THIS IS HOW TOUGH I AM!!!

ANCHOR

TA DA!

VILLAGER BOY MONKEY D. LUFFY

HA HA HA! GET IT OVER WITH!
WHAT-EVER IT IS...
WHAT'S THAT PUP UP TO NOW?
CHUNK
?!

HUH!?
AAARGH!!!
RGH
YOU IDIOT! WHAT'D YOU DO THAT FOR!?
YEOWWW!!

A TOAST!!
TO LUFFY'S... COURAGE...
AND TO OUR GREAT VOYAGE!

HAR HAR HAR HAR! DRINK UP!
GROG! GROG! GROG! MORE GROG!
HEY THAT'S MY MEAT!!
NOT ANY MORE! I'M GONNA EAT IT!
HEY, STOP FIGHTING! YOU'LL SPOIL OUR FUN!
GYAHAR HAR HAR HAR HAR HAR

IT DIDN'T HURT A BIT!
LIAR! THAT WAS A FOOLISH THING TO DO!
I'M NOT THE LEAST BIT AFRAID OF GETTING HURT!! TAKE ME WITH YOU ON YOUR NEXT VOYAGE!!
I WANNA BE A PIRATE TOO!!!
ANCHOR

READ THIS WAY

YOU?! A PIRATE?! IMPOSSIBLE!!

HAHAHAHAHAHA

LUFFY, DO YOU KNOW WHY WE CALL YOU "ANCHOR"? BECAUSE YOU CAN'T SWIM-- YOU JUST SINK!! WHAT GOOD IS A PIRATE WHO CAN'T SWIM?

BUT IF I DON'T FALL OVERBOARD, THEN IT DOESN'T MATTER IF I'M AN ANCHOR!!

AND I'M A STRONG FIGHTER!

I'VE BEEN TRAINING!

MY PUNCH IS AS POWERFUL AS A PISTOL!

PIRATE CAPTAIN "RED-HAIRED" SHANKS

TA DA

READ THIS WAY

A PISTOL, EH?
IS THAT SO...
ARE YOU DOUBTING ME?!

CALM DOWN, LUFFY!

LET'S JUST HAVE A GOOD TIME!

YEAH! PIRATES ALWAYS HAVE A GOOD TIME!

THE SEA IS VAST AND THERE'S LOTS OF ISLANDS TO EXPLORE!

AND BEST OF ALL, PIRATES HAVE **FREEDOM!!**

WOW!

YOU GUYS STOP FILLING HIS HEAD WITH CRAZY IDEAS.
BUT IT'S TRUE!
RIGHT!?

READ THIS WAY

C'MON, CAP'N...
LET'S TAKE THE LAD WITH US JUST THIS ONCE...
AYE!
YEAH!
OKAY, BUT ONE OF YOU WILL HAVE TO STAY BEHIND...
SORRY, LADDY, YOU'VE JUST BEEN BEACHED! LET'S DRINK!
HARHARHARHARHARHAR
HEY!! I THOUGHT YOU GUYS WERE ON MY SIDE!

YOU'RE JUST TOO YOUNG, KID.
MAYBE IN 10 YEARS I'LL GIVE YOU A CHANCE.
CAP'N SHANKS! I'M TELLING YOU...
I'M NOT A LITTLE KID!!

DON'T GET UPSET NOW. HERE, HAVE SOME MILK.
OH BOY! THANKS!
GLUG GLUG
SEE! A REAL PIRATE WOULD NEVER DRINK MILK!!
AR HAR HAR HAR HAR HAR
GRRR!
THAT WAS A DIRTY TRICK!

HMPH! I'M GETTING TIRED OF THIS.
I EVEN STABBED MYSELF IN THE FACE SO YOU'D TAKE ME WITH YOU.
LUFFY...
THE CAPTAIN'S JUST DOING WHAT'S BEST FOR EVERYONE...
FSSST
HOW DO YOU FIGURE, MR. FIRST MATE?

THE SAFETY OF THE ENTIRE CREW AND SHIP RESTS ON HIS SHOULDERS.
BEING A PIRATE ISN'T ALL FUN AND GAMES, YOU KNOW...
THERE'S LOT'S OF DUTIES LIKE... PILLAGING, HOSTAGE-TAKING, HEAVY DRINKING... AND SWIMMING!
?

AND THE CAPTAIN KNOWS ALL ABOUT THE DANGERS OF THE SEA, TOO!
IT CAN KILL YOU IN A THOUSAND WAYS!
IT'S NOT THAT HE WANTS TO CRUSH YOUR DREAM OF BECOMING A PIRATE.
WELL I DON'T BELIEVE IT!!
SHANKS JUST LIKES TO MAKE ME LOOK DUMB.
HEY, ANCHOR!
I TOLD YOU!
HAR HAR HAR

CAPTAIN SHANKS! I'M GLAD TO SEE YOU AND YOUR CREW ARE ENJOYING YOURSELVES.
HO BOY... I JUST LOVE MAKING FUN OF THIS KID!
HMM... MAYBE THE LAD'S GOT A POINT...
ANCHOR
MAKINO PROPRIETOR OF THE TAVERN
LUFFY, WOULD YOU LIKE SOMETHING TO EAT?
YEAH! JUST PUT IT ON MY TREASURE TAB!
TREASURE TAB? LOOK BOY, DON'T TRY TO SWINDLE THE LADY.
I'M GONNA BECOME A PIRATE, FIND LOTS OF TREASURE, AND THEN I'LL COME BACK AND PAY HER!!
THUMP
HA HA HA! WE'LL CELE-BRATE TO-GETHER WHEN YOU RETURN.
HEE HEE
HA HA

SHANKS...
YEAH KID...?
MUNCH MUNCH
CHOMP CHOMP
HOW MUCH LONGER WILL YOU STAY AT THIS VILLAGE?
SITOOB

HMM... LET'S SEE...
WE'VE BEEN USING THIS VILLAGE AS OUR BASE FOR ABOUT A YEAR...
CHOMP
KLNK
AFTER TWO OR THREE MORE VOYA-GES...
...WE'LL LEAVE HERE FOR GOOD AND HEAD NORTH.
I SEE...
ANCHOR

TWO OR THREE MORE TRIPS, EH?
HMM...

...

I'M GONNA LEARN HOW TO SWIM BY THE TIME YOU LEAVE!
THAT'S GOOD KID...
DO WHATEVER YOU WANT.

SLAM!!

!

KLAK-A-KLAK!!

MAKE WAY FOR THE SCOURGE OF THE MOUNTAINS!

HEH HEH... SO YOU CALL YOUR-SELVES PIRATES, EH?
FIRST TIME I'VE SEEN PIRATES... YOU LOOK LIKE A SORRY LOT TO ME.

?

...!
TMP
KLOMP

WE'RE MOUNTAIN BANDITS.
HIGUMA THE BEAR
LEADER OF THE MOUNTAIN BANDITS
TAP
OH, DON'T WET YOURSELVES. WE'RE NOT HERE TO BUST UP THE PLACE. JUST SELL US 10 BARRELS OF GROG, AND WE'LL INJURE ONLY THE BARE MINIMUM.
I'M SORRY...
WE JUST RAN OUT OF LIQUOR.
HMMM...
THAT'S STRANGE. WHAT'RE ALL THESE PIRATES DRINKING?
FRUIT JUICE?
IT'S TRUE...
I JUST SERVED THE LAST OF IT.

READ THIS WAY

I FEEL KINDA GUILTY...
I GUESS WE DRANK UP ALL THE LIQUOR.
SORRY ABOUT THAT.

WHY DON'T YOU HAVE THIS?
IT'S STILL UN-OPENED.

...

KRACK!
?!!
TINK TINK!!

WHAT DO YOU TAKE ME FOR?
WHAT GOOD IS ONE BOTTLE OF GROG?
YOU CAN'T MAKE A FOOL OF ME!
DRIP
DRIP

OH MY...
WHAT A MESS.

FWIP
WANTED
8,000,000
LOOK AT THIS.

MY HEAD'S WORTH 8,000,000 BERRIES.
I'M A WANTED MAN.
I'VE KILLED 56 PEOPLE...
MOSTLY FOOLS LIKE YOU!

WATCH YOURSELF... IF YOU'RE FOND OF BREATH-ING!
IF YOU'RE SMART YOU'LL SAIL AWAY FROM HERE SO I NEVER SEE YOU AGAIN.
WANTED

KLINK

READ THIS WAY

SORRY ABOUT THIS MESS, MAKINO.
GIVE ME A RAG AND I'LL CLEAN UP.
UH...
DON'T WORRY ABOUT IT.
SHHK!!
...

!

CRASH!!

!!!

SO, YOU LIKE TO CLEAN?
THAT OUGHT TO KEEP YOU BUSY FOR A WHILE.
HMPH!

FAREWELL.

...COWARDS.

NO GROG! THAT'S AN OUTRAGE!
PARTYS BAR
LET'S GO TO ANOTHER VILLAGE.

CAPTAIN, ARE YOU OKAY?
ARE YOU HURT?
I'M FINE. NO HARM DONE.

PHEW!!

HAR HAR HAR HAR! CAP'N!
HAR HAR HAR HAR HAR
HE GOT YOU GOOD!

READ THIS WAY

HA HA HA HA!

HUH?
YOU THINK IT'S FUNNY?!

HE MADE YOU LOOK LIKE A WEAKLING!!! WHY DIDN'T YOU FIGHT HIM?!

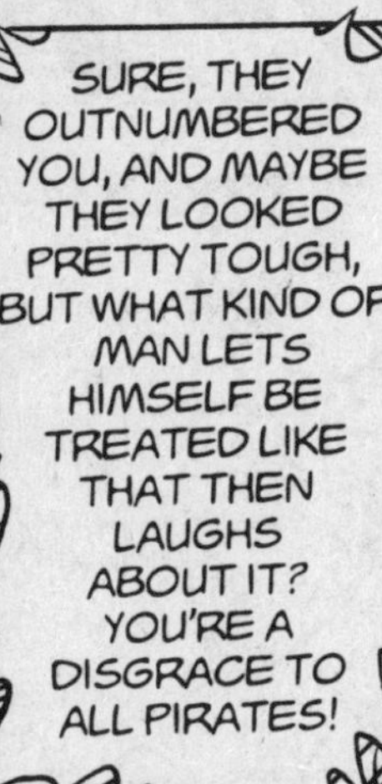
SURE, THEY OUTNUMBERED YOU, AND MAYBE THEY LOOKED PRETTY TOUGH, BUT WHAT KIND OF MAN LETS HIMSELF BE TREATED LIKE THAT THEN LAUGHS ABOUT IT? YOU'RE A DISGRACE TO ALL PIRATES!

...

WHEN YOU GROW UP MAYBE YOU'LL UNDER-STAND, KID.
HE JUST GOT SOME GROG ON ME, THAT'S ALL. NEEDLESS KILLING DOESN'T MAKE YOU A MAN.

HEY, WHERE YOU GOING?
HMPH! TO GO FIND A REAL ROLE MODEL!
STOMP
GRAB

!!??

PFFSH!!

HEY!!!

BWOING!

WHAT!!?

HIS ARM'S STRETCHING!!!

DOES THIS MEAN... DID HE--

HE COULDN'T HAVE!

!!

WHAT'S WRONG WITH ME?!!!

IT'S NOT HERE!!

HUH?!

THE GUM-GUM FRUIT WE TOOK FROM THAT ENEMY SHIP!!!

LUFFY! YOU DIDN'T EAT THAT FRUIT, DID YOU!?

!

YEAH...I ATE IT FOR DESSERT!!

IT DIDN'T TASTE ALL THAT GREAT, THOUGH...

WHAAAAAAAAAT!?
AAARGH!!
AAAHHHH
YOU IDIOT!!!!!
HHA
!
IF YOU EAT IT, YOUR ENTIRE BODY BECOMES LIKE RUBBER! AND YOU WILL NEVER BE ABLE TO SWIM FOR THE REST OF YOUR LIFE!
THAT WAS THE GUM-GUM FRUIT!!
THE FRUIT OF THE DEVIL, IT'S ONE OF THE SECRET TREA-SURES OF THE SEA!

TMPTMPTMP
MOO

HEY, MR. FISH MONGER!
GIVE ME SOME FISH!
SMIRK!
TA DA!
FISH MONGER
UO

HEY, RUBBER BOY! WHY ARE YOU IN SUCH A GOOD MOOD LATELY!

THE PIRATES SET SAIL WITHOUT YOU TODAY, YOU KNOW?

AND YOU WON'T BE ABLE TO SWIM ***FOR THE REST OF YOUR LIFE.***

IT DOESN'T MATTER. IF I SINK LIKE AN ANCHOR, THEN I'LL JUST BE A PIRATE THAT NEVER FALLS OVERBOARD!

I'M GLAD I ATE THE GUM-GUM DEVIL FRUIT...

BOOOING

LOOK AT WHAT I CAN DO!

YOU THINK BEING GAWKED AT BECAUSE YOU'RE A FREAK IS A GREAT THING, EH?

WELL, THIS VILLAGE DOESN'T NEED ANY MORE IDIOTS, SONNY!

GOOD MORNING, MR. MAYOR!

TA DA

FOR THE LAST TIME, LUFFY, I WON'T ALLOW YOU TO BECOME A PIRATE!

IT'D MAKE THE VILLAGE LOOK BAD!!

NOW, THE CAPTAIN'S NOT SUCH A BAD FELLOW, BUT YOU STAY AWAY FROM THOSE PIRATES!

BLAH

BLAHBLAH

BLAH

READ THIS WAY
PARTYS BAR
THE PIRATES HAVE BEEN OUT AT SEA FOR A LONG TIME.
DO YOU MISS THEM, LUFFY?
AFTER THE WAY THOSE MOUNTAIN BANDITS HUMILIATED THEM?! NOT AT ALL!

I REALLY MIS-JUDGED THOSE GUYS!
I THOUGHT THEY WERE BRAVE AND TOUGH... BUT THEY'RE REALLY JUST A BUNCH OF WIMPS.
TMP TMP
ARE YOU SURE ABOUT THAT?
MAYBE SOME-TIMES IT TAKES MORE COURAGE NOT TO FIGHT.

YOU JUST WOULDN'T UNDERSTAND, MAKINO.
A REAL MAN HAS TO STAND UP FOR HIMSELF, NO MATTER WHAT.
IS THAT RIGHT? I GUESS I DON'T UNDER-STAND.
THAT'S RIGHT. YOU DON'T.
?
MAKE WAY FOR THE TERROR OF THE HIGHLANDS!

READ THIS WAY

!!

WHA...

BA
NO PIRATES TODAY, EH? SMELLS BETTER...
WE WERE IN THE AREA, SO WE STOPPED BY.

WHAT'RE YOU WAITING FOR?
WUMP
!
WE'RE CUSTOMERS!!
SLAM!

SERVE US DRINKS!!!

SLAM!
MAYOR! WE'VE GOT A PROBLEM!
!

WHAT'S WRONG, MAKINO!

IT'S LUFFY...
AND THE MOUNTAIN BANDITS!

YOU'VE GOT A STRANGE BODY, BOY.
OUR PUNCHES AND KICKS AREN'T HURTING YOU AT ALL.
PARTYS BAR
!!

HEY! WE GOTTA GO HELP LUFFY!
ARE YOU CRAZY? THOSE MOUNTAIN BANDITS WOULD KILL US!
BESIDES, LUFFY'S THE ONE THAT STARTED THE FIGHT!

DARN YOU!!!
YOU'D BETTER TAKE IT BACK!!!
BWOING
YOU JERK!
THERE SURE ARE SOME WEIRD CREATURES IN THE WORLD...
EH, RUBBER BOY?
!
BWOING BWOING!!
OOF!
DARN YOU!!!
I'VE DIS-COVERED A NEW LIFE FORM...
I'LL MAKE YOU SO SORRY FOR THIS!!
MAYBE I'LL SELL YOU TO A FREAK SHOW...
I BET THEY'LL PAY GOOD MONEY FOR YOU.

YAAAAAAH!!
ROAR!
YOU STUBBORN LITTLE...
...BRAT!!
!
STOMP!
I WAS JUST DRINKING AND TALKING TO MY MEN.
I DIDN'T SAY ANYTHING TO OFFEND YOU.
!!!
YES YOU DID!!
YOU'D BETTER APOLOGIZE!!!

CURSE THAT LUFFY!

WHY'D HE HAVE TO PICK A FIGHT WITH THOSE GUYS?!

MOVE YOUR FOOT...

YOU STINKING MOUNTAIN APE!!!

LET THE BOY GO!

PLEASE!!

!

I DON'T KNOW WHAT LUFFY DID...

AND I HAVE NO INTENTION OF FIGHTING YOU PEOPLE...

BOW

BUT IF IT'S MONEY YOU WANT, YOU'LL GET IT.

JUST DON'T HURT THE BOY!

!

MAYOR!

NICE TRY, OLD MAN...

YOU KNOW HOW THE WORLD WORKS.

READ THIS WAY

BUT I'M AFRAID IT'S TOO LATE.
NO ONE CAN SAVE THIS BRAT NOW.
HE'S DONE THE UNPARDONABLE... HE ATTACKED ME...

AND HE CALLED ME NAMES.
BWANG BWANG
I CAN'T TAKE THAT FROM THIS LITTLE RUBBER-SPINED FREAK!
...

YOU STARTED THIS, BANDIT!
YOU MOUNTAIN MACAQUE!

THAT DOES IT. I'M NOT GONNA SELL YOU.
I'M GONNA KILL YOU!
SHHRR
!

LUFFY!
PLEASE! FORGIVE HIM!

NOBODY CAME TO GREET US AT THE HARBOR.
I WAS WONDERING WHAT WAS GOING ON...
!

LUFFY! I THOUGHT YOUR PUNCH WAS AS POWERFUL AS A PISTOL.

CAPTAIN SHANKS!!

OH, IT'S YOU MOUNTAIN BANDITS AGAIN!

COME ANY CLOSER AND WE'LL HAVE TO KILL YOU... COWARDS.
I DON'T KNOW WHAT YOU WANT, BUT YOU'D BETTER BACK OFF BEFORE YOU GET HURT.
...

NOT NOW, CAP'N!!
!!

HMPH! YOU PIRATES ARE STILL HERE?
TAKING A BREAK FROM YOUR CLEANING DUTIES?

READ THIS WAY

DIDN'T YOU HEAR HIM?! DON'T COME ANY CLOSER...
KLIK
...OR I'LL BLOW YOUR HEAD OFF! HA HA HA HA!!
SSH

HEH HEH HEH HEH!!

YOU'RE PUTTING YOUR LIFE ON THE LINE BY POINTING THAT AT ME.
HUH?! WHAT'RE YOU TALKING ABOUT?

I'M SAYING IT'S NOT SAFE TO POINT GUNS.

BOOM
!

SWUMP!!!
WHA--!!
...
...!
NOW YOU'VE GONE AND DONE IT!
WHAT'VE YOU DONE?!
THAT WASN'T FAIR!
FAIR?!
STOP WHINING LAND-LUBBERS!
YOU'RE NOT DEALING WITH SAINTS HERE.

WE'RE PIRATES!
AND WE DON'T PLAY BY THE RULES!

THIS WAS NONE OF YOUR BUSINESS!
LISTEN UP...
YOU CAN POUR DRINKS ON ME, YOU CAN THROW FOOD AT ME...
YOU CAN EVEN SPIT ON ME. I'LL JUST LAUGH THAT STUFF OFF.
BUT...

GOOD REASON OR NOT...
NOBODY HURTS A FRIEND OF MINE!!!!

FRIEND?!
HA HA HA HA!
NICE SPEECH, VERY INTIMIDATING!

YOU PIRATES SPEND YOUR TIME FLOATING AROUND IN YOUR LITTLE SHIPS.

AND YOU THINK YOU CAN STAND UP TO MOUNTAIN BANDITS? DON'T MAKE ME LAUGH!

KILL THEM!

ARRRRGHH!

ARRRGG

DIE!!!!

CAP'N...

I'LL TAKE CARE OF THIS.

TSSS...!!
!
YAAAAA!!!
NEXT...
YEOOWWW!!!
WHACK!

YOU WERE SAYING SOMETHING ABOUT MOUNTAIN BANDITS AND PIRATES?
FSST
KA
KLIK

WOW, HE'S STRONG!
WOW...

IF YOU WANNA FIGHT US...
YOU BETTER BRING A BATTLESHIP.
...!
PARTYS BAR

BUT...
...THE BRAT STARTED IT!

DOESN'T MATTER. THERE'S A PRICE ON YOUR HEAD, ISN'T THERE?

...

!?
HMPH!
SMOKE BOMB!!!
POOF!!
LUFFY!!
C'MERE KID!!
HEY! LET GO!
OH NO! I LET HIM ESCAPE! WE'VE GOTTA SAVE LUFFY!!
CALM DOWN, CAPTAIN! WE'LL ALL GO OUT AND LOOK FOR HIM! WE'LL FIND HIM!!
HMM...
CAP'N...

HA HA HA HA HA!
WHAT A BRILLIANT ESCAPE!
AND NOBODY WOULD EVER EXPECT A MOUNTAIN BANDIT TO HIDE OUT AT SEA!!

I BROUGHT YOU ALONG AS A HOSTAGE...
BUT I NO LONGER HAVE A USE FOR YOU!
I'VE ALREADY KILLED 56 PEOPLE WHO WERE FOOLISH ENOUGH TO MAKE ME MAD, WHAT'S ONE MORE?
!!
YOU DIE!
UNH
PWANG

TSK TSK
GOODBYE...
BWOINK!
...!!

#%&!!
JERK!!
BRAT...
THAT GUY IS SCUM!
AND I DIDN'T EVEN GET ONE PUNCH IN! DARN IT!
!!!
&%$#!!!!
HA HA HA HA HA!!
DID YOU SEE THE LOOK ON THOSE PIRATES' FACES?
HA HA HA HA HA
I BROKE A BOTTLE OVER HIS HEAD, AND NOT ONE WORD OF PROTEST!!
HOW PATHETIC!! HA HA HA HA!!
I WANTED TO KILL HIM!
COWARDS LIKE THAT MAKE ME SICK!
PIRATES ARE ALL TALK.
TAKE THAT BACK!
HUH!?
TAKE BACK WHAT YOU SAID ABOUT SHANKS!! HE'S NOT A COWARD!!
LUFFY! STOP!
STOP TALKING BAD ABOUT SHANKS!!!!

SPLASH!!
HA HA HA HA HA HA HA!!
SPLASH
GLUG GLUG
SPLASH!!
GLUG
?!!!
SPLASH
GRRRRR...
HUH?
WHAT... THE-- AAH!!
GYAAAAA!
CHOMP CHOMP
KRUNCH!!

GRR RR!!
YAAAA!!
GLUG GLUG!!
SPLASH
SPLASH
GLUG! SOMEBODY HELP ME!! GLUG!
YAAAAAAH!!!
CHOMP!!
CHOMP
CHOMP!!
SHANKS!

GR
RR
GET OUT OF HERE!
HRUNH
SPLASH SPLASH
....!!
SNIF
SPLASHSPLASH
REEREEREE
SPLOOSH
!!

LUFFY, I'M SORRY.
MAKINO TOLD ME WHAT HAPPENED.
SNIFFLE!
SNIF!
YOU STOOD UP FOR ME.
HEY, STOP CRYING! YOU'RE A TOUGH GUY, REMEMBER?
B-BUT...
SHANKS!!!
SNIF SNIF
WHAT ABOUT YOUR ARM!!?

IT'S A SMALL PRICE TO PAY...

JUST AN ARM...

I'M JUST GLAD YOU'RE OKAY.

WAAAAAH!

WAHHHHHHHHHHHHHHHHH WAAAAAH!

LUFFY UNDERSTOOD WHY SHANKS WOULDN'T TAKE HIM OUT TO SEA.
THE DANGERS OF THE SEA WERE TOO GREAT...
AND HE WAS NOT YET STRONG ENOUGH...
BUT MOST OF ALL, LUFFY REALIZED WHAT A GREAT MAN SHANKS WAS.
HE VOWED TO BE JUST LIKE HIM ONE DAY.

SO YOU WON'T BE COMING BACK TO THIS VILLAGE AFTER THIS VOYAGE?

THAT'S RIGHT.
WE'VE BEEN USING THIS HARBOR AS A BASE OF OPERATIONS FOR A LONG TIME. MAYBE TOO LONG.
ARE YOU SAD?

YEAH, I'M SAD...
BUT I WON'T ASK YOU TO TAKE ME WITH YOU!
I'VE DECIDED TO BECOME A PIRATE ON MY OWN!
IT WOULDN'T DO YOU ANY GOOD. YOU'RE STILL TOO LITTLE!
NYAH
THERE'S NO WAY YOU CAN BECOME A PIRATE!

OH YES I WILL!!!
ONE DAY I'LL HAVE A SHIP AND CREW BETTER THAN YOURS!!
AND WE'LL HAVE THE BIGGEST HOARD OF TREASURE IN THE WORLD!!

I'M GONNA BE KING OF THE PIRATES!!!

HMM... YOU'RE GONNA BE BETTER THAN US, HUH?

...
WELL THEN...

DO ME A FAVOR...

TMP

KEEP THIS HAT SAFE FOR ME?

!

THIS HAT MEANS A LOT TO ME.
...!!

PROMISE THAT YOU'LL GIVE IT BACK TO ME SOMEDAY...
...WHEN YOU'VE BECOME A GREAT PIRATE.

THAT KID'S GONNA MAKE SOME-THING OF HIMSELF.
YEAH...
HE ACTS JUST LIKE I DID WHEN I WAS A KID.
WEIGH THE ANCHOR!
RAISE THE SAILS! WE'RE OFF WITH THE TIDE!!

LUFFY'S ADVENTURE...
...BEGINS 10 YEARS LATER FROM THIS VERY SAME SPOT.

TA
TEN YEARS LATER...
DA!

WELL, HE'S FINALLY SETTING OUT, EH, MAYOR?
I'LL MISS THAT RASCAL.
BUT IF HE DOES BECOME A PIRATE, HE'LL BRING SHAME TO THE VILLAGE.
I NEVER THOUGHT HE'D REALLY DO IT!

IT'S A GOOD DAY TO SET OUT TO SEA!
WOW!
KREEK
KREEK
SKREE
SKREE

READ THIS WAY
GRRRR...
SPLOOSH
WHOA...
OUR LOCAL SEA MONSTER!
SORRY I HAVE TO DO THIS...
BUT HERE'S AN ATTACK I'VE BEEN PERFECTING SINCE THE LAST TIME WE MET!!
GUM-GUM...

...PISTOL!!!

SPLOO
HMPH!
THAT'S WHAT YOU GET, YOU DARN FISH!

FLEX FLEX
HMM...
FIRST THINGS FIRST. I'VE GOT TO GET A CREW!
I THINK ABOUT 10 MEN SHOULD DO.

AND I'LL NEED A PIRATE FLAG!!

LOOK OUT WORLD, HERE I COME!
I'M GOING TO BECOME...
...THE KING OF THE PIRATES!!!!
LUFFY'S TINY BOAT FLOATS ON, HIS CREW YET TO BE FOUND...
LUFFY'S GREAT VOYAGE OF DESTINY HAS BEGUN!!!

ONE PIECE
PIRATE CAPTAIN
RED-HAIRED SHANKS
FIRST MATE
ANCHOR
LUFFY AS A BOY

WOW! WHAT A GREAT DAY!
SKREE
SKREE
THIS IS NO ORDINARY BOY IN A ROWBOAT. THIS IS A BOY WITH A DREAM, CHALLENGING THE VAST, TREACHEROUS SEAS IN A TINY DINGHY, SEARCHING FOR EXTRAORDINARY MEN FOR HIS PIRATE CREW!
THE WEATHER'S SO NICE!
WHO'D HAVE THOUGHT THIS VOYAGE WOULD END IN DISASTER SO SOON?
MONKEY D. LUFFY
CHAPTER 2: THEY CALL HIM "STRAW HAT LUFFY"

WHRRR
HARD TO BELIEVE THAT I'M GETTING SUCKED INTO THIS GIANT WHIRL-POOL...
MAYBE I WAS A LITTLE CARELESS...

SHWRRR
WMMMMMMM
TOO BAD I CAN'T SWIM, TOO.
SHWRRR
I COULD USE SOME HELP, BUT THERE'S NOBODY AROUND.
OH WELL, CAN'T BE HELPED. DOWN I GO...

AAAA!
SPLOOSH
YIKES!!
HA! WHAT WAS I THINKING? IN A GIANT WHIRLPOOL, IT DOESN'T REALLY MAKE A DIFFERENCE IF YOU CAN SWIM OR NOT!
I'D DROWN EVEN IF I COULD SWIM!

CHAPTER 2:
THEY CALL HIM "STRAW HAT LUFFY"

KER-PLOOSH

AN UN-CHARTED ISLAND...

WHY IS THERE DUST ON MY BULWARK?
SHWIK
DA-DUM

A THOUSAND PARDONS, LADY ALVIDA!!
I-I THOUGHT I'D CLEANED EVERY INCH OF THIS SHIP...!!
I'LL CLEAN EVERY-THING ALL OVER AGAIN! PLEASE--!
"PLEASE" WHAT...?

READ THIS WAY

PLEASE, NOT THE IRON MACE!!
I-I DON'T WANNA DIE!!!
WONK!
!!
KOBY! **WHO** IS THE **FAIREST** THROUGHOUT **ALL** THE SEAS?
FWUMP
AHEM... HEH HEH... WHY **YOU** ARE... LADY ALVIDA!!
NO ONE COMPARES TO YOU!!

CORRECT!! WHICH IS WHY I WILL NOT TOLERATE **ANYTHING** DIRTY!!
WHOOOO
THE SHIP I SAIL IN MUST BE AS CLEAN AND BEAUTIFUL AS I AM. UNDERSTAND?

REMEMBER, KOBY, WERE IT NOT FOR YOUR VAST **KNOWLEDGE** OF THE SEAS, I WOULD FEED YOU TO THE SHARKS! BUT DON'T PUSH YOUR LUCK!
Y-YES... THAT'S VERY **KIND** OF YOU.
KLAK KLAK KLAK
OTHER THAN THAT, YOU'RE **WORTHLESS!** HERE, SHINE MY SHOES!!
WHAM WHAM
Y-YES, LADY ALVIDA! RIGHT AWAY!
EEEK

I DON'T WANT TO SEE EVEN ONE SPECK OF DUST ON THIS SHIP!!!
AYE AYE!
THE LADY PIRATE
IRON MACE ALVIDA
DWA
THAT'S ENOUGH!! YOU'RE PATHETIC!!
WUMP
OOF!
HEH HEH HEH... SORRY...
IF YOU'VE GOT TIME TO GROVEL, THEN YOU'VE GOT TIME TO SCRUB THE TOILET!!
HEH HEH...
YES, MILADY! RIGHT AWAY...

...RIGHT AWAY...
...
SLUMP

WHAT'S *THAT,* KOBY? DID A BARREL OF RUM WASH UP ON THE BEACH?
Y-YEAH. AND IT'S NOT EMPTY! I WASN'T SURE WHAT TO DO WITH IT...
ROLL
WELL *I* KNOW WHAT TO DO WITH IT! LET'S DRINK IT ALL UP!
BUT IF THE CAPTAIN FINDS OUT, SHE'LL HAVE OUR HEADS!
SHE'LL NEVER FIND OUT!

WE'RE THE ONLY ONES HERE.
JUST KOBY AND THE THREE OF US KNOW ABOUT THIS.
I GUESS YOU'RE RIGHT.
AND YOU AIN'T SEEN NOTHIN', RIGHT, KOBY?
RIGHT! I-I AIN'T SEEN NOTHIN'! HEH HEH HEH
GRR
PLEASE DON'T HIT ME...

WHAT THE DEVIL!?
THAT WAS A GREAT NAP!!!
HMM... LOOKS LIKE I SURVIVED SOMEHOW.
I GOT SO DIZZY I THOUGHT I WAS GONNA BARF!! HAHAHAHA!

HMMM?
....!?
HUH!?
....!?
WHO ARE YOU GUYS?
WHO THE HECK ARE YOU!!?
WHAT WERE YOU DOING IN THERE!?
BACK TO WORK, YOU SCURVY DOGS!!!
WOOSH
WHOOSH
ARRGH!
WABAM!!
ARRGH!
!!!

WHOOSH
WHOA!
KRASH
OH!

TWEET
....!!
TWEET

YOU LAZY SWABBIES! WHO'S THE FAIREST THROUGHOUT ALL THE SEAS?
LADY ALVIDA! YOU ARE... OF COURSE!

AND YOU DARE TO DEFY ME?
?
W-WHAT!? NEVER! NOT IN A MILLION--

LOOM

DON'T PLAY DUMB WITH ME! I COULD HEAR YOU TALKING ALL THE WAY FROM THE SHIP!
WHICH ONE OF YOU HAD SUCH A "GREAT NAP"!

YAAAWWN!!!
TA-DA!
THAT WAS A GREAT NAP!!!
GASP!

READ THIS WAY

UH... CAPTAIN! WE HAVE AN INTRUDER!!
YEAH! THAT GOOD FOR NOTHIN' KOBY BROUGHT THAT STRANGE FELLER HERE!
WHAT!? COULD HE BE A BOUNTY HUNTER...
...AFTER THE PRICE ON MY HEAD?
KOBY! YOU TRAITOROUS LITTLE RUNT!

BUT THE ONLY BOUNTY HUNTER BOLD ENOUGH TO COME HERE...
THAT'S RIDICULOUS!! THE NAVY HAS HIM LOCKED UP...

BUT IF HE'S AS CLEVER AS THEY SAY... HE MIGHT'VE ESCAPED!
AND THEY SAY THAT THE INFAMOUS RORONOA ZOLO IS THAT CLEVER!!

UM... ARE YOU OKAY? ARE YOU HURT?
AFTER GETTING KNOCKED AROUND SO MUCH YOU MUST BE-
HA HA HA HA!
I'M FINE, JUST A LITTLE SURPRISED IS ALL.
MY NAME'S LUFFY! WHERE AM I?

READ THIS WAY

THIS ISLAND IS THE HIDEOUT OF IRON MACE ALVIDA, THE LADY PIRATE.
I'M KOBY, HER CABIN BOY.
KOBY THE CABIN BOY
I SEE...
WELL, NONE OF THAT REALLY MATTERS TO ME.
OH...

YOU WOULDN'T HAPPEN TO HAVE A DINGHY, WOULD YOU? MINE GOT SUCKED INTO A GIANT WHIRLPOOL.
YOU GOT SUCKED INTO A GIANT WHIRLPOOL!?
YEAH, IT CAUGHT ME BY SURPRISE!
PHEW
YOU'RE LUCKY TO BE ALIVE!
...BUT IF IT'S A DINGHY YOU WANT, I HAVE ONE... SORTA...

WHAT'S THIS!?
HUH!!
A COFFIN?
I BUILT IT MYSELF. IT TOOK ME TWO YEARS...
TWO YEARS!? AND YOU DON'T WANT IT?

...I REALLY DON'T NEED IT ANYMORE. I BUILT IT TO ESCAPE FROM THIS PLACE...
...BUT I DON'T HAVE THE COURAGE TO TRY IT. I GUESS IT'S MY FATE TO BE A CABIN BOY FOR THE REST OF MY LIFE.
BUT I *ONCE* HAD A DIFFERENT DREAM.
WHY DON'T YOU JUST ESCAPE?
N-NO WAY! JUST THINKING ABOUT WHAT ALVIDA WOULD DO TO ME IF SHE CAUGHT ME MAKES MY BLADDER WEAK...
NOPE NOPE NOPE NOPE
I JUST CAN'T RISK IT...
NOPE NOPE NOPE NOPE

I'LL NEVER FORGET THAT FATEFUL DAY... I JUST WANTED TO GO FISHING...

...AND I BOARDED A PIRATE SHIP BY MISTAKE.

TA DUM DABADA DUM

THAT WAS TWO YEARS AGO. IN EXCHANGE FOR MY LIFE, I'VE BEEN WORKING AS THEIR CABIN BOY.

SIGH

YOU'RE KINDA CLUMSY AND DUMB!

AND YOU'RE GUTLESS TOO. YOU REALLY ARE **WORTHLESS!**
HA HA HA
YOU DON'T HAVE TO BE *THAT* FRANK...
EHEH HEH HEH...
WHIMPER
BUT YOU'RE RIGHT. I DON'T HAVE THE GUTS TO FLOAT AROUND AT SEA IN A BARREL LIKE YOU...
LUFFY, WHY DID YOU GO TO SEA ANYWAY?

WELL, YA SEE...
SMIRK
I'M GONNA BE THE KING OF THE PIRATES!!!
K-KING OF THE PIRATES!!!?
BUT... YOU'D HAVE TO MAKE THE WHOLE WORLD KNEEL TO YOU!!!
WEALTH, FAME, POWER-- YOU'D HAVE TO ACHIEVE IT ALL!!!
DON'T TELL ME YOU'RE AFTER GOLD ROGER'S LOST TREASURE, "ONE PIECE"!!!!...

DO YOU WANT TO DIE!?
EVERY PIRATE IN THE WORLD IS AFTER THAT!!
AND SO AM I.
BUT THE ODDS AGAINST YOU ARE ASTRONOMICAL!!?
NEVER NEVER NEVER
YOU WANT TO BE THE KING OF THE PIRATES IN THE GOLDEN AGE OF PIRACY!?
IT'S IMPOSSIBLE!!
IT'LL NEVER HAPPEN!!
HEY!
W-WHY'D YOU HIT ME!?
YOU WERE HYSTERICAL.
KLONK
OKAY, I'M USED TO IT.
HEH HEH HEH...
I'M NOT AFRAID TO DIE, KOBY!
HUH!?
I'VE SET MYSELF TO BECOME THE KING OF THE PIRATES...
AND IF I DIE TRYING... THEN AT LEAST I TRIED!
!!!
WHAT GUTS... WHAT DETERMINATION!!
Y-YOU'RE NOT EVEN AFRAID TO DIE!?

AND I BELIEVE I'LL SUCCEED, TOO.
OR AM I JUST DELUDING MYSELF...
...
I NEVER LOOKED AT IT LIKE *THAT* BEFORE!!
...!!
SNIFF
MAYBE... I CAN BE LIKE THAT!
SNIFF
IF I'M WILLING TO RISK MY LIFE TRYING...
HUH?
...MAYBE IT'S POSSIBLE!
DO YOU THINK I CAN JOIN THE NAVY!?
THE NAVY!?
WE'LL END UP BEING ENEMIES...
BUT I WANT TO JOIN THE NAVY AND FIGHT THE BAD GUYS!!
IT'S BEEN MY DREAM SINCE I WAS A LITTLE KID!!

LUFFY! DO YOU THINK I CAN DO IT?
HOW WOULD I KNOW?
WELL, I'M GONNA DO IT!!!
WHAT'VE I GOT TO LOSE!? I DON'T WANNA BE A MISERABLE CABIN BOY MY WHOLE LIFE!!
BETTER TO RISK MY LIFE TRYING TO ACHIEVE MY DREAM!
I'LL JOIN THE NAVY... AND THEN... I'LL CAPTURE ALVIDA!!
WHO ARE YOU GOING TO CAPTURE, RUNT!?
AAAH!!!
KRESH!!
!
!!
MY BOAT!
YOU LITTLE SNEAK!
DID YOU REALLY THINK YOU COULD ESCAPE FROM ME!?

ANSWER ME!!!
WHO IS THE ***FAIREST*** THROUGHOUT ALL THE SEAS?
SO I'LL GIVE YOU ***ONE CHANCE*** TO REPENT...
DA-DUM.....!!
IS ***THAT*** THE BOUNTY HUNTER YOU HIRED? WELL, HE CERTAINLY ISN'T ***RORONOA ZOLO...***
ZOLO?
...!

BWAAA
HEY, WHO'S THAT TOUGH-LOOKING OLD BIDDY?
!!!!

HEH HEH HEH...
LADY ALVIDA, YOU--

THROUGHOUT ***ALL*** OF THE SEAS, LADY ALVIDA IS...
LUFFY!! TAKE IT BACK!!
NO WAY!
HOW DARE...

LADY ALVIDA IS...
I'M GONNA BE THE KING OF THE PIRATES...
AND IF I DIE TRYING... THEN AT LEAST I TRIED!
LADY ALVIDA IS...
...THE UGLIEST OLD HAG OF ALL!!!
SHAAAOOO
GULP!
HA HA HA HA HA HA!
AHA HA HA
YOU LITTLE--!!!
I SAID IT AND I **WON'T** TAKE IT BACK! NO MORE CRINGING FOR ME!! FROM NOW ON, I'LL FIGHT FOR MY DREAMS!!
EYAAA!

FUNK
L-LUFFY...!!
GOOD FOR YOU, KOBY!!
IT MAKES NO DIFFER-ENCE TO ME...
YOU'RE BOTH GOING TO DIE!!
!!
THAT DIDN'T HURT!
'CAUSE I'M MADE OF RUBBER!
IMPOSSIBLE! NO ONE SURVIVES THE IRON MACE!!
!!?
SMIRK

YOU'VE GOTTA BE KIDDING!
!?
GUM-GUM...
...PISTOL!
WHAT THE--?
!!!?
WOM!!

H-HIS ARM STRETCHED LIKE RUBBER...
CAPTAIN!!!
HE BEAT LADY ALVIDA! HE'S NOT HUMAN!
GIVE KOBY A DINGHY!
HE'S GONNA JOIN THE NAVY!
Y-YESSIR...
HA HA HA!
PLOP PLOP
LUFFY...

YOU MUST HAVE EATEN THE FRUIT OF THE GUM-GUM TREE...

INCRED-IBLE!

BUT LUFFY, IF YOU'RE GOING AFTER ***ONE PIECE...***

THAT MEANS YOU'LL HAVE TO ENTER THE "GRAND LINE."

YEP!

THEY CALL IT THE **PIRATES' GRAVEYARD...**

THAT'S WHY I'M ASSEMBLING A ***SUPER CREW.***

THAT GUY IMPRISONED AT THE NAVY BASE...

WHAT'S HIS NAME?

RORONOA ZOLO!

IF HE'S A GOOD GUY, I'LL LET HIM JOIN MY CREW!

NOW YOU'RE TALKING CRAZY AGAIN!

NEVER NEVER NEVER! THAT'LL ***NEVER*** HAPPEN! THAT GUY'S A DEMONIC BEAST!

HOW DO ***YOU*** KNOW!?

NEVER!

AND SO THE TWO YOUNG ADVENTURERS SAIL ON TOWARDS THE NAVAL BASE AND... DESTINY!

STEP 1
THE PIRATE FLAG
"THE SKULL AND CROSSBONES" - THE CROSSBONES ARE THIGH BONES.

HERE IS SOME INFORMATION REGARDING THE PIRATE FLAG. THE PIRATE FLAG IS GENERALLY CALLED THE "JOLLY ROGER" AND IS A SYMBOL OF DEATH. SCARY, ISN'T IT?

THERE ARE MANY THEORIES CONCERNING THE ORIGIN OF THE TERM "JOLLY ROGER."

⚜ SOME SAY IT COMES FROM THE FRENCH "JOLIE ROUGE" OR "RED LOVELY," POSSIBLY REFERRING TO BLOOD.

⚜ ANOTHER POSSIBILITY IS THAT "ROGER" WAS ORIGINALLY THE WORD "ROGUE," MEANING A THIEF OR VILLAIN.

⚜ AND THEN THERE ARE THOSE WHO SAY IT'S RELATED TO "OLD ROGER," WHICH WAS A NAME FOR THE DEVIL.

THE DEVIL

CHAPTER 3: ENTER ZOLO–PIRATE HUNTER

...A DEMONIC BEAST, HUH?
RORONOA ZOLO IS HIS REAL NAME...
BUT THEY CALL HIM "ZOLO THE PIRATE HUNTER."

HE'S LIKE A BLOODTHIRSTY HOUND...
...ROAMING THE SEAS, HUNTING MEN FOR THE BOUNTIES ON THEIR HEADS!
THEY SAY HE'S A DEMON IN HUMAN FORM.

HMMM...
LUFFY, HE'S A PIRATE HUNTER! PIRATE HUNTERS DON'T MIX WELL WITH PIRATES!

I HAVEN'T DECIDED WHETHER I'LL INVITE HIM TO JOIN MY CREW OR NOT.
IF HE'S A GOOD GUY, THEN I'LL—
HE'S IN PRISON BECAUSE HE'S **NOT** A GOOD GUY!!

CHAPTER 3 :
ENTER ZOLO: PIRATE HUNTER

DA—DUM
MARINE
WE'RE FINALLY HERE! WE MADE IT TO THE NAVAL BASE TOWN.
YEAH! WE FINALLY MADE IT!
KOBY, YOU'RE AMAZING!
HUH?
TA-DA
YOU ACTUALLY GOT US TO OUR DESTINATION!
OF COURSE I DID!
THAT'S THE MINIMUM REQUIREMENT FOR PEOPLE WHO SAIL THE SEAS.
LUFFY, IF YOU KEEP RANDOMLY FLOATING AROUND, YOU'LL NEVER BECOME A PIRATE.
YOU SHOULD FIND A NAVIGATOR FOR YOUR CREW.
YEAH!! THAT'S WHAT I'LL DO!! NOW, LET'S EAT!!

READ THIS WAY

FOOD FOO

WELL, KOBY, I GUESS THIS IS WHERE WE GO OUR SEPARATE WAYS.

I HOPE YOU JOIN THE NAVY AND BECOME A GREAT SAILOR!

TH-THANK YOU, LUFFY!

AND I HOPE YOU BECOME A GREAT PIRATE!

...EVEN IF THAT MEANS WE'LL BE ENEMIES.

HEY, I JUST REMEMBERED... THAT GUY IS SUPPOSED TO BE IMPRISONED HERE-- RORONOA ZOLO...

KRASH!!

!!!

TRMBL TRMBL
...?
....!!!
MAYBE YOU SHOULDN'T SAY THAT NAME OUT LOUD AROUND HERE...
PSST PSST
HMMM...

I SAW A POSTER THAT SAID THAT CAPTAIN MORGAN IS AT THIS BASE.
KRATA-KRASH
!!!
HUH!?
WOW!!
HA HA HA HA! WHAT A GREAT RESTAU-RANT!
I WANT TO GO BACK THERE AGAIN!
HA HA HA HA HA!
EVERYONE IS SO JUMPY! I'M GETTING A BAD FEELING ABOUT THIS!
I CAN UNDERSTAND WHY THEY GET NERVOUS WHEN THEY HEAR RORONOA ZOLO'S NAME -- HE MIGHT ESCAPE AT ANY MOMENT!
BUT WHY DID THEY GET NERVOUS HEARING THE CAPTAIN'S NAME?
WHO KNOWS!? MAYBE THEY JUST GOT CARRIED AWAY!
WHY WOULD THAT HAPPEN!?
I'M TRYING TO THINK SERIOUSLY HERE...

DA-DUM!!

NAVY BASE

MARINE

MARINE 海軍

...!

IT LOOKS SO BIG UP CLOSE!

GO ON IN, KOBY!
B-BUT I HAVEN'T MENTALLY PREPARED MYSELF YET...
AND THOSE PEOPLE SURE WERE SCARED WHEN THEY HEARD THE CAPTAIN'S NAME...

LUFFY! WHAT'RE YOU DOING!?
SHUMP

I WONDER IF I CAN SEE...
...THE DEMONIC BEAST FROM HERE.

MAYBE IT'S ZOLO!
GULP
WHAT!?
OH YEAH? WELL THERE'S SOMEBODY OVER THERE!
HE'S PROBABLY DEEP WITHIN THE BOWELS OF THE PRISON...
YOU WON'T FIND HIM JUST BY PEEKING OVER THE FENCE.

SHAAOOO

THERE HE IS!
LUB-DUB LUB-DUB
...
SNEAK...

WHAT'S WRONG!?
I-IT'S REALLY HIM! THAT'S RORONOA ZOLO!!!
A B-BLACK BANDANNA AND A HARAMAKI SASH!!!
LUB-DUB LUB-DUB
HE LOOKS SO... MENACING!!!

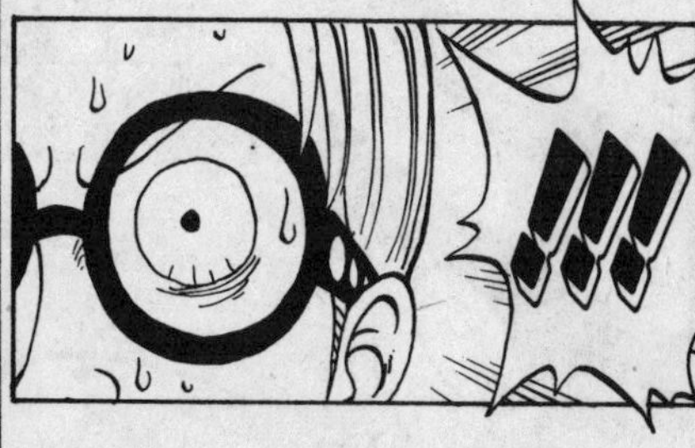
!!!

MARINE
SO THAT'S HIM. HMM! I COULD JUST UNTIE THOSE ROPES AND SET HIM FREE...

YIKES!
HUH?
HEY, KID!

IF YOU LET HIM LOOSE, HE'LL KILL US THEN WRECK THE TOWN!!
THAT'S SUICIDE!!

I'VE BEEN HERE FOR NINE DAYS AND I CAN'T TAKE ANYMORE.
SHAAOOO
COME OVER HERE...
...AND UNTIE ME...
I'LL MAKE IT WORTH YOUR WHILE.
I'LL CAPTURE SOMEONE WITH A BIG PRICE ON THEIR HEAD AND GIVE ALL OF THE BOUNTY TO YOU.
YOU CAN TRUST ME. I'M A MAN OF MY WORD.
H-HE'S TALKING TO US!!
HEY! HE'S SMILING!

D-DON'T DO IT, LUFFY!
AS SOON AS YOU UNTIE HIM, HE'LL KILL US AND GET AWAY! I JUST KNOW IT!
HE WON'T KILL US.
HE COULDN'T.
I WOULDN'T LET HIM!

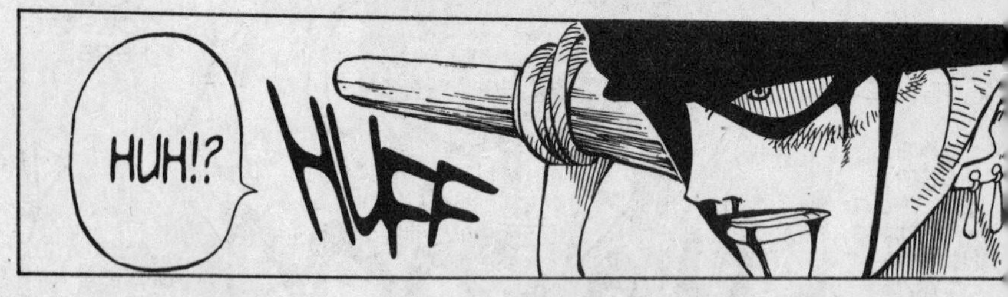
HUFF
HUH!?

WHAT A BIG HEAD HE'S GOT!

HUH!?
HUH!?
SHHH!

WHAK

HEY! D-DON'T GO DOWN THERE! IT'S DANGEROUS!
TMP TMP...
?
WHADDA YOU WANT?

LUFFY! DO SOMETHING! SHE'LL BE KILLED!
WHY DON'T YOU DO IT YOUR-SELF?

GET LOST! DO YOU WANT TO GET KILLED!?

I MADE THESE RICE BALLS FOR YOU! I THOUGHT YOU MIGHT NEED SOME FOOD!

IT'S THE FIRST TIME I'VE EVER MADE RICE BALLS. I HOPE YOU LIKE THEM.
I'M... NOT HUNGRY!!
NOW BEAT IT AND TAKE THAT STUFF WITH YOU!!

B-BUT...
I DON'T WANT IT!! NOW GET OUTTA HERE!!
OR I'LL STOMP YOU TO DEATH!!

!
I'LL TELL MY FATHER ON YOU!
KLANK
!
YOU SHOULDN'T PICK ON LITTLE GIRLS.
RORONOA ZOLO!!!
HELMEPPO CAPTAIN MORGAN'S SON
WHO'S THAT WEIRDO?
HE MUST BE SOME HIGH RANKING NAVAL OFFICER.
NOW THAT LITTLE GIRL WILL BE SAFE.
HMPF!
WELL... IF IT ISN'T THE IDIOT SON, LIVING OFF DADDY'S WEALTH.
DID YOU JUST CALL ME AN "IDIOT"?
A MAN IN YOUR POSITION SHOULD GUARD HIS TONGUE... OR HE COULD LOSE IT!

LITTLE GIRL...

SNATCH

DID YOU BRING THOSE RICE BALLS FOR ME? HOW THOUGHTFUL.

HEY! GIVE IT BACK!

BLECH!

DISGUSTING! IT'S SWEET! THERE'S SUGAR ON IT!

HYAK

RICE BALLS ARE SUPPOSED TO BE SEASONED WITH SALT! NOT SUGAR!!

B-BUT I LIKE SWEETS, SO I FIGURED SUGAR WOULD BE BETTER!

THESE ARE COMPLETELY INEDIBLE!!

SPLAK

STOP! PLEASE! YOU'RE RUINING THEM!

SPLAK

SPLAK

HOW EVIL... THAT LITTLE GIRL WORKED REALLY HARD TO MAKE THOSE RICE BALLS.

DON'T WORRY! I'M SURE THE ANTS FIND THEM DELICIOUS!
HA HA HA!
KWISH
KWISH
HA HA!
OH NO!
SKWISH
....!

WHY!!! I WORKED SO HARD TO MAKE THEM!!
PLOP PLOP
OH, STOP THAT CRYING!
THAT'S WHY I HATE KIDS!
HMPF!

IT'S YOUR OWN FAULT!
CAN'T YOU READ THIS SIGN?
MARINE
ANYONE AIDING THIS PRISONER SHALL BE FOUND GUILTY OF THE CRIMES HE HAS COMMITTED. —CAPTAIN MORGAN
IT SAYS, "ANYONE AIDING THIS PRISONER SHALL BE FOUND GUILTY OF THE CRIMES HE HAS COMMITTED.
—CAPTAIN MORGAN"
...!!!
I'M SURE YOU'VE HEARD HOW SCARY MY FATHER CAN BE!
IF YOU WERE AN ADULT, YOU WOULD BE PUT TO DEATH!
SNFF

YOU THERE! THROW THAT BRAT OVER THE FENCE!!
B-BUT...
ARE YOU GOING TO DISOBEY A DIRECT ORDER!?
I'M ORDERING YOU TO THROW THAT LITTLE BRAT OVER THE FENCE!
I'LL TELL DADDY ON YOU!
Y-YES SIR... RIGHT AWAY!!

YAAHHH!!

!

SPLOING

...!!

ARE YOU OKAY!?
WHAT A BAD MAN...!
...
BRUSH BRUSH

MY, AREN'T YOU A STUBBORN ONE!
THAT'S RIGHT, I'M GONNA LAST OUT THE ENTIRE MONTH!
YOU JUST KEEP YOUR END OF THE BAR-GAIN!

HA HA HA! I WON'T DREAM OF BREAKING MY WORD.
IF YOU SURVIVE OUT HERE FOR A MONTH, THEN I'LL LET YOU GO!!
HA HA HA
SHUF SHUF
IT'S MY PLEA-SURE, I'M SURE!!

READ THIS WAY

!
YOU STILL HERE?
BETTER NOT LET HELMEPPO'S FATHER CATCH YOU.
LOOK...

I'M LOOKING FOR GOOD MEN TO JOIN MY PIRATE CREW.
PIRATE CREW?
YOU THINK I'D LOWER MYSELF TO THAT LEVEL? NO THANKS!
MARINE
BUT BECOMING A PIRATE'S MY DREAM!
WHAT'S WRONG WITH IT!?

YOU THINK IF YOU UNTIE ME...
I'M GONNA JOIN YOUR PIRATE CREW?

I HAVEN'T DECIDED IF I'LL ASK YOU YET...
YOU'VE GOT A PRETTY BAD REPU-TATION, YOU KNOW?

BAD REPUTATION, HUH?
WELL, ANYWAY, I DON'T GO FOR THAT KIND OF DEAL.
I'VE GOT MY OWN PLANS FOR THE FUTURE.
I DON'T NEED YOUR HELP. I CAN GET OUT OF HERE ON MY OWN.
ALL I HAVE TO DO IS LAST FOR A MONTH HERE, THEN I'M A FREE MAN!
CAPTAIN MORGAN'S IDIOT SON PROMISED ME.
ALL I'VE GOT TO DO IS SURVIVE HERE FOR ONE MONTH.
THEN I'LL BE FREE TO PURSUE MY DREAM!!!
HMM... I SEE.
I DON'T THINK I COULD LAST ***ONE WEEK*** WITHOUT FOOD.
ME AND YOU ARE DIFFERENT. I'VE GOT MORE WILL POWER.
SO GO LOOK FOR A CREW ELSEWHERE...
HEY, WAIT A MINUTE...
HUH?
PICK THAT UP FOR ME.

YOU'RE NOT GOING TO EAT IT!?
IT'S MORE OF A DIRT BALL THAN A RICE BALL NOW...
I KNOW YOU'RE HUNGRY, BUT THIS--
SHUT UP!
AAH!
JUST SHUT UP AND FEED IT TO ME!
AND DON'T MISS ONE GRAIN OF RICE!

MNCH MNCH MNCH
CHOMP
MNCH
...!
CHOMP!
...!
HAK KOFF KOFF!!!
!!!
I TOLD YOU. IT WAS MOSTLY DIRT. YOU WANNA KILL YOURSELF?
KOFF... T-TELL THE KID...
TWITCH
TWITCH
HUH?

TELL HER I SAID IT WAS DELICIOUS.
TELL HER I ATE IT ALL.
!
HA HA HA!

COULD THAT GUY REALLY BE AS BAD AS EVERYONE SAYS?
HE'S *NOT* A BAD GUY!
I'M SO GLAD!
YEAH!
HE ATE IT ALL UP!
REALLY!?

RORONOA ZOLO SAVED ME! BESIDES, THOSE DOGS WERE RUNNING LOOSE AND SCARING EVERYBODY IN TOWN!
CAPTAIN MORGAN'S SON HAD A BUNCH OF MEAN DOGS! THEY ATTACKED ME...
HE GOT THROWN INTO PRISON 'CAUSE OF ME.
BUT HE HASN'T DONE ANYTHING WRONG!
EVERYBODY IN TOWN IS AFRAID OF HIM...

AND HE WOULDN'T GET THROWN INTO PRISON FOR THAT!
ZOLO'S REALLY SCARY, BUT HE ONLY GOES AFTER PEOPLE WITH A PRICE ON THEIR HEADS.
THAT MAKES SENSE!
YES!
THAT'S WHY ZOLO IS IN PRISON...
BECAUSE HE HURT THAT GUY'S DOG TO SAVE YOU?

CAPTAIN MORGAN AND HIS SON ARE THE BAD ONES!
THEY PUT PEOPLE TO DEATH FOR NO REASON AT ALL! EVERYONE'S AFRAID OF THEM.
HA HA HA! YOU'RE NOT BOWING YOUR HEADS LOW ENOUGH, SCUM! I'LL TELL MY FATHER ON ALL OF YOU!!
!

DO YOU WANT TO BE JAILED LIKE RORONOA ZOLO!?
WE'RE GOING TO HOLD A PUBLIC EXECUTION FOR HIM IN THREE DAYS!!
HAHAHA
WE'LL MAKE AN EXAMPLE OF HIM! I CAN HARDLY WAIT!
STOMP STOMP
THREE DAYS?

BUT... YOU MADE A PROMISE TO HIM!?
WHAT? WHERE DID YOU HEAR ABOUT THAT?
GASP
GASP
THAT PROMISE WAS JUST A JOKE!!
HE'S JUST A STUPID BEAST FOR BELIEVING IT!!
PFFT~!!
HA HA HA!
CAPTAIN MORGAN'S IDIOT SON PROMISED ME. ALL I'VE GOT TO DO IS SURVIVE HERE FOR ONE MONTH.

AAAH!
!!!!
AAAAH!
LUFFY!!
STOP! CALM DOWN!!
THAT GUY IS SCUM!
AAAH!
WAAAH!
YOU WANT TO MAKE AN ENEMY OF THE NAVY, DO YOU!?
HAAAH!
WAAA
KOBY, I'VE MADE MY DECISION!
HUH?
I'M GOING TO ASK ZOLO TO JOIN MY CREW!!!

HOW TO DRAW THE SKULL AND CROSSBONES

1. DRAW A CIRCLE.

2. DRAW THREE CIRCLES INSIDE THE CIRCLE.

3. DRAW ANOTHER CIRCLE BELOW THE FIRST CIRCLE.

4. DRAW TWO LINES ACROSS THE LOWER CIRCLE.

5. DRAW THREE VERTICAL LINES ALONG THE HORIZONTAL LINES.

6. DRAW BONES BEHIND THE SKULL.

TA-
-DA

7. AND YOU'RE FINISHED! WHAT!? WAIT A MINUTE...

8. AND YOU'RE FINISHED!

9. AND IF YOU DRAW A STRAW HAT ON IT, YOU GET LUFFY'S FLAG!

CAPTAIN MORGAN WILL BE FURIOUS!
HE PUNCHED THE CAPTAIN'S SON!
GASP!!
H-HE REALLY DID IT!!

NO ONE HAS EVER HIT ME! NOT EVEN DADDY!

Y-YOU HIT ME! YOU ACTUALLY HIT ME!

WSS

SCUM IS SCUM... NO MATTER WHO ITS FATHER IS!

WSS

WSS

LUFFY! STOP! ARE YOU TRYING TO PICK A FIGHT WITH THE WHOLE NAVY!

CHAPTER 4:

THE GREAT CAPTAIN MORGAN

I'M CAPTAIN MORGAN'S BELOVED SON!!!
I'M TELLING DADDY ON YOU!
GASP!!!
DON'T RUN CRYING TO PAPA! FACE ME LIKE A MAN!
LUFFY! PLEASE STOP!
YOU'LL DIE BEGGING FOR MERCY!
YOU'RE A WALKING CORPSE!
FATHER WILL KILL YOU!
HE'S NOT WORTH HITTING.
YOU BOOGER-FACE!!
TMPTMPTMP
POF
NOW YOU'VE DONE IT...

YOU WERE GREAT, BIG BROTHER!
I FEEL A LOT BETTER NOW!
THEN I WISH I'D GIVEN HIM A FEW MORE WHACKS FOR YOU!
RIKA!!
GET OVER HERE!

YOU SHOULDN'T BE TALKING TO THAT PERSON!
IF THEY THINK YOU'RE HIS FRIEND, THEY'LL KILL YOU, TOO!!
BUT, MOMMY, HE'S A GOOD MAN. AND ZOLO, HE'S A GOOD--
SLAM, SLAM
...
WHAT ARE YOU SAYING!? YOU DIDN'T GO TO THE PARADE GROUND, DID YOU!?
UM... WELL... NO-O-O...

HURRY UP, LET'S GET INSIDE...
SLAM
THEY WON'T LET YOU GET AWAY WITH THIS!
AND CAPTAIN MORGAN HAS THE WHOLE NAVY BEHIND HIM!
AAAAAAAA
YEAH, WHATEVER. I NEED TO TALK TO ZOLO.

NAVAL FORTRESS
MARINE
MARINE
PHOO...

I'M SO...
DA-DOOM
...GREAT!!

YES SIR!
YOU CERTAINLY ARE, SIR! YOU'RE THE GREAT CAPTAIN MORGAN, SIR!
THEN WHY ARE THE TRIBUTES FROM THE PEASANTS... AHEM... TOWNS-FOLK...
YESSIR, REGARD-ING YOUR TRIBUTES...
...I BELIEVE THE TOWNS-PEOPLE ARE NOW TOO POOR TO RAISE--
MARINE

...GETTING SMALLER!?
MARINE

IT'S NOT A QUESTION OF HOW MUCH THEY CAN PAY...
IT'S A QUESTION OF THEIR RESPECT FOR ME!

DADDY!!
WHAT'S WRONG, HELMEPPO? WHY THE COMMOTION?
SLAM!!

I WANT YOU TO KILL SOMEONE FOR ME!!

HEY!
YOU AGAIN...
IF THIS IS ABOUT ME JOINING YOUR PIRATE CREW, MY ANSWER IS STILL NO!

CALL ME LUFFY!
I'LL UNTIE YOU IF YOU'LL JOIN MY PIRATE CREW, OKAY!?
YOU DON'T LISTEN, BOY!

READ THIS WAY

I'VE GOT MY OWN MISSION...
...AND IT DOESN'T INVOLVE BECOMING A STINKING PIRATE!

YOU'RE TOO GOOD TO BE A PIRATE?
YOU, A BOUNTY HUNTER? WHO EVERYONE THINKS IS SOME SORT OF DEMON?

I DON'T CARE WHAT PEOPLE THINK.
I LIVE BY MY OWN CODE... I'VE NEVER DONE ANYTHING I REGRET, AND I DON'T INTEND TO IN THE FUTURE.

WHICH IS WHY I'LL NEVER BE A PIRATE!!
...

I HEARD YOU CAN USE A SWORD!
!...
HMPH! IF I WASN'T TIED UP, I'D SHOW YOU...

SORRY, BUT I'VE MADE UP MY MIND! YOU'RE GONNA JOIN MY CREW!!
I DON'T CARE WHAT YOU'VE DECIDED!!

READ THIS WAY

SO WHERE ARE YOUR SWORDS NOW?
THEY TOOK 'EM FROM ME. THE CAPTAIN'S IDIOT SON...
NEXT TO MY LIFE, THOSE SWORDS ARE MY DEAREST TREA-SURES.

HMM...
TREASURES, HUH? TOO BAD THEY TOOK 'EM...

I KNOW!
I'LL GET YOUR SWORDS FROM THE IDIOT SON!!
WHAT?

THEN, IF YOU WANT YOUR SWORDS BACK...
YOU'LL HAVE TO JOIN MY CREW!
YOU LITTLE RAT!
HA HA HA

HEY! COME BACK!!
SEE YA SOON!

HE'S GOING INTO THE FOR-TRESS...
THAT'S ONE DUMB PIRATE!

OKAY! STEADY!
STAND IT UP!

FATHER!! WHY AREN'T YOU HUNTING THE BRIGAND WHO HIT ME!!
EVEN YOU NEVER LAID A HAND ON MY LOVELY-YET-MASCULINE FACE BEFORE!
DO YOU KNOW WHY I'VE NEVER HIT YOU?
BECAUSE I'M YOUR BELOVED S--
I'LL TELL YOU WHY...

IT'S BECAUSE YOU'RE AN IDIOT SON WHO'S NOT EVEN WORTH HITTING!!

ARF!!

WHY SHOULD I FIGHT YOUR BATTLES?
YOU'RE BIG ENOUGH TO WIPE YOUR OWN BOTTOM...
I DON'T MIND IF YOU USE MY STATUS...
BUT I ONLY LAY HANDS ON PEOPLE WHO DEFY ME!!!
DON'T FOOL YOURSELF...
YOU ARE NOT THE GREAT ONE! I AM GREAT!!
I AM THE GREAT ONE.
...!
NAVAL CAPTAIN "AXE-HAND" MORGAN
DA-WM!

I HEARD A LITTLE MOUSE SNUCK INTO MY PARADE GROUND.
THE LITTLE GIRL?
I DEALT WITH HER. I--
SO YOU KILLED HER.
MÖWE

WHAT!?
NO... I, UH... SHE WAS JUST A LITTLE GIRL AND I...
SHE DIDN'T EVEN KNOW WHAT SHE WAS DOING...
YOU! FIND HER AND KILL HER!
HUH!?
CHILD OR NOT, ANYONE WHO DEFIES ME MUST SUFFER THE PENALTY!

BUT, CAPTAIN, SHE'S JUST A LITTLE GIRL...
I WOULDN'T OBEY SUCH A CRUEL ORDER!
OH, WOULDN'T YOU? YOU ARE A LIEUTENANT IN THE NAVY AREN'T YOU?
AND I-- A CAPTAIN-- AM YOUR SUPERIOR OFFICER, AM I NOT?
UH... YES SIR...
MARINE

THEN YOU ARE DUTY-BOUND TO OBEY ME!!
IF I SAY KILL HER, THEN YOU WILL KILL HER!!
I...
I WON'T MURDER A LITTLE GIRL!!
MUTINY!
AAAAAAAA!!
GASP
YOU DIDN'T HAVE TO KILL HIM!!
LIEUTENANT!!
NO MATTER. THE TOWNSFOLK MUST BE TAUGHT *RESPECT*.
I'LL HANDLE IT PERSONALLY!

FOR YEARS I LABORED TO ACHIEVE THIS RANK, AND I DID IT BY MY OWN STRENGTH... AT GREAT PERSONAL COST!
MY RANK IS THE HIGHEST ON THIS BASE...
WHICH MAKES ME SUPERIOR TO EVERYONE ELSE HERE...
RANK MEANS *EVERYTHING* IN THIS WORLD, REMEMBER THAT!
THAT MEANS EVERYTHING I DO IS RIGHT!!!
IS THAT CLEAR?
YES SIR!!
YOU ARE THE GREATEST, SIR!
FWAP!
THIS IS A MONUMENT TO MY RANK AND POWER!!!
IT TOOK YEARS TO BUILD, BUT TODAY IT IS FINALLY COMPLETE.
BAM!
OOOO
KREEK
KREEK
RAISE MY STATUE! PUT IT AT THE HIGHEST POINT OF THIS FORTRESS AS A SYMBOL OF MY GREATNESS!!

NO ONE TO HELP ME FIND ZOLO'S SWORDS...
...OR THE IDIOT SON...
THAT'S FUNNY... THERE AREN'T ANY SAILORS AROUND...
MAYBE THEY'RE HAVING A MEETING OR SOME-THING...
MARINE

WHAT WAS THAT!?
DID YOU JUST BUMP IT!?
SORRY, SIR! WE WERE CARELESS, SIR!

KLUNK
UNH!

HEAVE!! HEAVE!!

BRRCH !!
I'LL JUST CHECK IT OUT!

HUH?
I THINK I HEAR VOICES UP THERE.
MARINE

KTCH
BOOM
UNH!
BANG
GWOING
GUM-GUM...
FWUP!!
...ROCKET!!!

THIS STATUE IS LIKE MY PERSON!
SCRATCHING IT IS THE SAME AS ATTACKING ME!
SWINE! DO YOU KNOW HOW LONG I'VE WAITED FOR THIS STATUE TO BE FINISHED!?
AND YOU'VE ALREADY SCRATCHED IT!!
SORRY, SIR! I'LL PAY TO HAVE IT FIXED!
FOOSH
LET THIS BE A WARNING TO ALL!
AAAAH!
BWRRRM
GOT IT!
FRAP
HUH!?
!
WHOA!
I OVER-SHOT!
WHAT'S THAT!?
IT CAME FROM BELOW!!
MARINE
MARINE
MARINE

KRAKOOM
WOW...
MARINE
MARINE
MARINE
!!!!!
MARINE

UM...
SORRY.

KRAKASH

ROWRR

SEIZE HIM! I'LL HAVE HIS HEART!!!

YES SIR!!

AYE AYE, SIR!!

DADDY!!

THAT'S THE RUFFIAN WHO HIT ME! IF YOU HAD KILLED HIM THIS WOULD NEVER HAVE--

I'VE BEEN LOOKING FOR YOU!!
L-LET ME GO! FATHER! HELP!!
HE'S ENTERING THE FORTRESS!
HELP ME!
GET HIM!

CAPTAIN! SOMEONE'S IN THE PARADE GROUND!!
WHAT!!?
HFF HFF
ALL THESE REBELS DEFYING ME! KILL 'EM ALL!

WHAT!? LUFFY WENT INTO THE FOR-TRESS!?
WHY IS HE SO RECKLESS!?
YEAH, I'VE NOTICED. WHO IS HE ANYWAY?
HEY! NOW ***YOU'RE*** BEING RECKLESS! IF THEY CATCH YOU FREEING ME, THEY'LL KILL YOU!
THEY IMPRISONED YOU UNFAIRLY!
I CAN'T STAND TO SEE THE NAVY ACT IMPROPERLY.
I'M GOING TO BECOME A PROPER SAILOR! JUST LIKE LUFFY'S GOING TO BE THE KING OF THE PIRATES!

WHAT!?
KING OF THE PIRATES!? DOES HE KNOW WHAT THAT MEANS!?

HA HA HA... I WAS SHOCKED WHEN HE FIRST TOLD ME, TOO.
BUT HE'LL SUCCEED OR DIE TRYING! THAT'S HOW HE IS!

BOOM
!

MARINE

THERE HE IS! GET HIM!
WHERE ARE ZOLO'S SWORDS!?
I-I'LL TELL YOU! JUST STOP DRAGGING ME!
KRFF
BUMP BUMP

MAKE YOUR OWN ORIGINAL PIRATE FLAG!

HAVE YOU MASTERED THE BASICS OF THE SKULL AND CROSSBONES? NEXT, WE'LL SHOW YOU HOW TO CREATE YOUR OWN ORIGINAL DESIGNS!

EXAMPLES

LUFFY'S FLAG
Just add a straw hat!

SHANKS' FLAG
Add three scars on the left eye and replace the crossbones with swords.

ALVIDA'S FLAG
In profile with a heart symbol.

SUGGESTIONS

If you like baseball you can do something like this!

...Or like this, if you want to be a cook!

Here's another original design!

CHAPTER 5: THE KING OF THE PIRATES AND THE MASTER SWORDSMAN

RRK!!
OKAY, TELL ME!

TELL ME! WHERE ARE ZOLO'S SWORDS!?
BUMP
BUMP
S-STOP DRAGGING ME AND I'LL TELL YOU!
BUMP

YOU SHOULD'VE TOLD ME! YOU'RE WASTING TIME!
OUCH! YOU HIT ME AGAIN!

THEY'RE IN MY ROOM!
HFF
WE PASSED IT A LONG WAY BACK.
HFF

I DON'T WANT TO.

DROP THE CAPTAIN'S SON OR WE'LL SHOOT!
KLIK
!

READ THIS WAY

HUH?
PWIP
OKAY! GO AHEAD AND SHOOT!
KLOMP KLOMP KLOMP
AAAAH!
DON'T SHOOT! DON'T SHOOT!
HE'S USING HELMEPPO AS A SHIELD!!

WAAAAH!
WAAAAH!

AAAAAAH!
AAAH!!
I'VE BEEN SHOT! AAAAH!
WUB-DUB WUB-DUB
BLOOD! I'M BLEEDING!! AAAH!!

READ THIS WAY

I'M GONNA DIE!!!

...
GOOD! YOU'RE ALIVE!
PHEW

NOW GET OUTTA HERE!
THEY'RE ON THEIR WAY DOWN.

HFF HFF...
HFF
HFF
BUT... HFF HFF... I HAVEN'T UNTIED YOU...

DON'T WORRY ABOUT ME. I JUST HAVE TO SURVIVE THE MONTH AND THEY'LL LET ME GO.
SO JUST BEAT IT--
THEY'RE NOT GOING TO LET YOU GO!
YOU'RE GOING TO BE EXECUTED THREE DAYS FROM NOW!!
WHAT ARE YOU SAYING!? THAT IDIOT PROMISED ME! IF I SURVIVE HERE FOR A MONTH, I'LL BE SET FREE!!

HE NEVER INTENDED TO KEEP THAT PROMISE!
NAAH!
HFF
HFF
THAT'S WHY LUFFY PUNCHED HELMEPPO!
BECAUSE HE FOUND OUT HELMEPPO LIED TO YOU!!

...!
WHAT!?

THE NAVY IS YOUR ENEMY NOW!!
HFF
HFF
PLEASE! IF I UNTIE YOU, WILL YOU HELP LUFFY!?

HE SAVED MY LIFE! I WON'T ASK YOU TO BECOME A PIRATE, BUT...
...

LUFFY'S REALLY STRONG AND SO ARE YOU! IF YOU TEAM UP...
...YOU CAN ESCAPE FROM HERE! PLEASE, HELP HIM!

STAY WHERE YOU ARE!
!!?
CAPTAIN MORGAN HAS ORDERED YOUR IMMEDIATE EXECUTION!!!
MARINE

SLA
THIS MUST BE THE ROOM!

HEY!
THE SWORDS!

READ THIS WAY

BUT THERE ARE THREE SWORDS!?
WHICH ONES ARE ZOLO'S?

HUH? HE FAINTED?
CHOKE
HMM?

WHAT'S GOING ON DOWN THERE!?

!
KOBY!

SURROUND THE FORTRESS!! IF THAT RASCAL IN THE STRAW HAT ESCAPES, YOU'LL ALL BE SORRY!!!!

AHA!!
YOU THREE AREN'T SIMPLE OUTLAWS, ARE YOU!?
YOU'RE TRYING TO OVERTHROW ME!!

RORONOA ZOLO! PEASANTS AND PIRATES MAY TREMBLE AT YOUR NAME... BUT YOU'RE NO MATCH FOR THE GREAT ONE!

YOU MAY BE A BARRACUDA...

BUT I'M A ***GREAT WHITE SHARK!***

TAKE AIM!

CHAK!!

!!!

I-I...

...

I CAN'T DIE YET!

THERE'S SOME-THING I HAVE TO DO...

ZOLO IS 0 FOR 2000 AGAINST KUINA!
OH WELL...
"TWO-SWORD ZOLO" LOSES!!
KUINA WINS AGAIN!!
UGH!
YAAH!
I MADE A PROMISE!
WAP!!
HE'S EVEN STRONGER THAN THE GROWN-UPS!
YEAH! HE'S THE STRONGEST IN OUR DOJO!
HEY! ZOLO'S NOT WEAK!
KIND OF WEAK FOR A BOY, AREN'T YOU?
PATHETIC...
SHE THINKS SHE'S SO GREAT JUST BECAUSE SHE'S THE SENSEI'S DAUGHTER!
KUINA MAKES ME SO MAD!
DARN!
SHE'S KINDA CUTE, THOUGH...
EVEN IF HE CAN USE TWO SWORDS, HE'S STILL WEAK!
LOSERS SHOULD LEARN TO SUFFER DEFEAT IN SILENCE.
THAT SO? WELL, HE'S NOT AS STRONG AS ME!

SENSEI! ARE YOU TEACHING HER SECRET TRICKS BECAUSE SHE'S YOUR DAUGHTER!?

OF COURSE NOT!

GRMBL GRMBL

IT'S NOT FAIR!

LOST AGAIN, EH, ZOLO?

IT'S ODD BECAUSE YOU ARE ACTUALLY VERY STRONG.

TA WA

SENSEI!

BUT I CAN BEAT **GROWN-UPS**!

DON'T FORGET THAT KUINA IS A LITTLE OLDER THAN YOU.

WHY CAN'T I BEAT THAT GIRL!?

KLATA KLAK

DARN!

I CAN'T KEEP LOSING TO THAT GIRL!
I'M GOING TO SAIL THE SEAS AND BECOME THE GREATEST SWORD MASTER IN THE WORLD!

HYAAH!
KLAK
KLAK
HYAAH!

HFF
HFF

ZOLO...
HFF

KUINA! I CHALLENGE YOU TO A DUEL... WITH REAL SWORDS!!
YOU'RE NOT AFRAID OF REAL SWORDS, ARE YOU?

REAL SWORDS? OKAY...

IT'S YOUR FUNERAL.

SKFF
SKFF

ON GUARD!

I'M READY!

UWAHH!!
YAAHH!!
CHING
CHING!
CHING..
CHING..
!!!
THAT MAKES 2001 TIMES I'VE BEATEN YOU!
THUNK
DAMN!
T'S
SO
RUS-
ATING!

I'M THE ONE WHO'S FRUS-TRATED...
HUH?
WHEN GIRLS GET OLDER, THEY BECOME WEAKER THAN THE BOYS.
PRETTY SOON YOU'LL ALL BE STRONGER THAN ME.
ZOLO, YOU'RE ALWAYS SAYING...
...THAT YOU'RE GOING TO BECOME THE WORLD'S GREATEST SWORDS-MAN...
DAD SAYS THAT GIRLS CAN'T BE MASTER SWORDSMEN...
...
YOU'RE LUCKY YOU'RE A BOY, ZOLO...
I WANNA BECOME THE WORLD'S GREATEST SWORDSMAN TOO!!
BUT I'M STARTING TO GET BREASTS...
I WISH I WAS A BOY...
WHAT ARE YOU CRYING ABOUT! YOU BEAT ME!!
THAT'S NOT FAIR! BEATING YOU IS MY DREAM!

I'M TRAINING ALL THE TIME TO BEAT YOU! YOU'RE MAKING ME LOOK BAD!
SOMEDAY I'LL BEAT YOU BECAUSE I WORKED HARD, NOT BECAUSE YOU GOT WEAKER!! IT'S GOT NOTHING TO DO WITH BEING A BOY OR A GIRL!!
ZOLO ...
LET'S MAKE A PROMISE TO EACH OTHER!
!
SOMEDAY, ONE OF US WILL BECOME THE GREATEST SWORDSMAN EVER!!
WE'LL FIGHT EACH OTHER FOR THE TITLE!
YOU IDIOT!
SNIFF
YOU'RE TOO PUNY!
IT'S A PROMISE!
SWAK!!

ZOLO! THERE'S BEEN AN ACCIDENT! IT'S KUINA!
SHE FELL DOWN THE STAIRS...
SHE'S DEAD!!!
MAN! YOU MADE A PROMISE YESTERDAY!
YOU CAN'T RUN AWAY FROM YOUR PROMISE!?
ZOLO! STOP IT!
HUMANS ARE FRAGILE THINGS, ZOLO...
SENSEI! MAY I HAVE HER SWORD?
...I SUPPOSE SO...
I'LL HAVE TO KEEP THE PROMISE FOR BOTH OF US.
I'M GOING TO BECOME SUCH A GREAT MASTER SWORDSMAN THAT MY NAME WILL BE KNOWN EVEN IN HEAVEN!!!!

I PROMISED HER!

I CAN'T DIE YET!!

GUM-GUM...
...ROCKET!!
KRASH

FIRE!!!
MÖWE
BWOINNG

!!!

BAP BAP BAP BAP

YOU!?

LUFFY!!!

STRAW HAT...

BREEEEN

UNGH!

BULLETS CAN'T HURT ME!!
LOOK OUT!!!
ZIP ZING
HA HA HA HA HA!!!

WHAT ARE YOU!?
GRG
GRG

I'M THE GUY...
WHO'S GONNA BE KING OF THE PIRATES!!!
TWNK

SO WHICH SWORDS ARE YOURS?
I DIDN'T KNOW, SO I BROUGHT ALL THREE...

THEY'RE ALL MINE.
I PRACTICE SANTORYU- THREE-SWORD STYLE.

IF YOU FIGHT THE NAVY WITH ME HERE AND NOW, IN THE EYES OF THE GOVERNMENT, YOU'LL BE ONE OF THE BAD GUYS!
...
OF COURSE, YOU COULD OBEY THE LAW... AND LET THEM KILL YOU!

YOU MUST BE DEMON SPAWN...
BUT I'M NOT READY TO DIE WITHOUT A FIGHT! ALL RIGHT!
YOU'VE GOT YOURSELF A PIRATE!!!

THE ROAD TO AXE-HAND MORGAN'S FIRST APPEARANCE

I created Helmeppo's character first, so my first thoughts when creating Captain Morgan were "He has to have a cleft chin and hair like Helmeppo's, only crazier—after all, he is the father."

TA—DA

This is what I came up with. Originally his name wasn't Morgan, it was "Chop." So his full title was "Naval Captain Chop" or "Sailor Chop." What a great name! But even I didn't have the nerve to use this name. [Editor's Note: "Sailor" in Japanese is *suihei*, and *Suihei Chop* is the name of a signature fighting technique used by the famous Japanese pro wrestler Giant Baba.]

I AM THE GREAT ONE!

I can't show them all here, but I actually made two or three more versions of Captain Morgan before I settled on the one used in the manga. I redesigned him to look cooler because a certain editor told me he looked lame. I couldn't argue with that, so I changed his look.

READ
THIS
WAY

REALLY!? YOU'LL JOIN MY CREW!?
YEAH!!
I DON'T HAVE MUCH CHOICE! NOW, UNTIE ME!!

WHAT IS HE!?
BULLETS BOUNCE RIGHT OFF HIM!
MARINE
MARINE
MARINE
MARINE

CHAPTER 6 :
NUMBER ONE

READ THIS WAY

HE'S NO ORDINARY HUMAN!!!
HE'S EATEN ONE OF THE DEVIL FRUIT...

...THE SECRET TREASURE FROM *THOSE* SEAS!!?
GASP
NO WAY! SO THAT'S HIS POWER...?
CAPTAIN! H-HE'S UNTYING ZOLO!!
WELL STOP HIM, YOU FOOLS!

IF BULLETS CAN'T HURT HIM, THEN USE YOUR SWORDS!

READ THIS WAY

UNH! THESE KNOTS ARE TOO TIGHT...

C'MON! HURRY UP!

I CAN'T UNTIE 'EM!

UNH...

HUH?

OOOH... WHERE AM I?

YIKES!

GASP!

WHAT!!?

NAAH

LUFFY!! ZOLO!! WATCH OUT!!!

I'M TRYING. JUST HOLD ON...

THERE'S NO TIME!!

THERE! I UNTIED ONE OF YOUR ARMS!

SNIP

GIVE ME MY SWORDS, MORON!!

THOSE WHO DEFY ME MUST DIE!!

...!!!

READ THIS WAY
KLANG!
!!!
MARINE
MARINE
MARINE
MARINE

READ THIS WAY

RORONOA ZOLO!!!
...!!

WOW!!
HE'S COOL!!

THE FIRST ONE WHO MOVES...
...DIES.

GA-CHEEN
EEEEK...!
HE'S SO SCARY...!

ALL RIGHT, SO I'M A PIRATE. I GAVE YOU MY WORD.
I'VE FOUGHT THE NAVY, THEREFORE I'M OFFICIALLY AN OUTLAW...
BUT, HEAR THIS!! I HAVE A MISSION TO FULFILL!!!
!

I'M GOING TO BE THE WORLD'S GREATEST SWORDSMAN!
ALL I HAVE LEFT IS MY DESTINY!
MY NAME MAY BE INFAMOUS...
...BUT IT'S GONNA SHAKE THE WORLD!!!

BUT YOU ARE MAKING ME BECOME A PIRATE! SO IF I HAVE TO ABANDON MY DREAM FOR ANY REASON...
...THEN I'M GOING TO MAKE YOU COMMIT HARA KIRI!!!

THE WORLD'S GREATEST SWORDSMAN, THAT'S GREAT!

AND IT'S FITTING SINCE YOUR NEW BOSS IS GOING TO BE THE KING OF THE PIRATES!

ANYTHING ELSE WOULD MAKE ME LOOK BAD!

GASP
HACK THOSE BRIGANDS INTO MINCE-MEAT! NOW!!
VWOOOSH
WHY DO YOU HESITATE!?
HMPH!
YOU TALK BIG...

ZOLO, DUCK!!
!
!!!
GUM-GUM...
FWOOSH

...WHIP!!!...
MAR

MARINE

!!?

WOW!
HE'S INCRED-IBLE!
WHAT THE DEVIL ARE YOU!?

I'M A...
...RUBBER MAN!!!

READ THIS WAY

A RUBBER MAN!?
CAPTAIN!! THEY'RE TOO MUCH FOR US!!
!!
IT'S HOPELESS! WE CAN'T FIGHT A RUBBER MAN...
...AND THAT DEMON RORONOA ZOLO AT THE SAME TIME!!

READ THIS WAY

HEAR ME!

ALL YOU COWARDS WHO WERE WHINING JUST NOW...

WILL SHOOT YOURSELVES IN THE HEAD!

!!!

I WON'T TOLERATE DEFEATISTS...

...IN MY OUTFIT!!!

ON MY ORDER... FIRE!!

GASP!

...!!
KACHAK
!!!

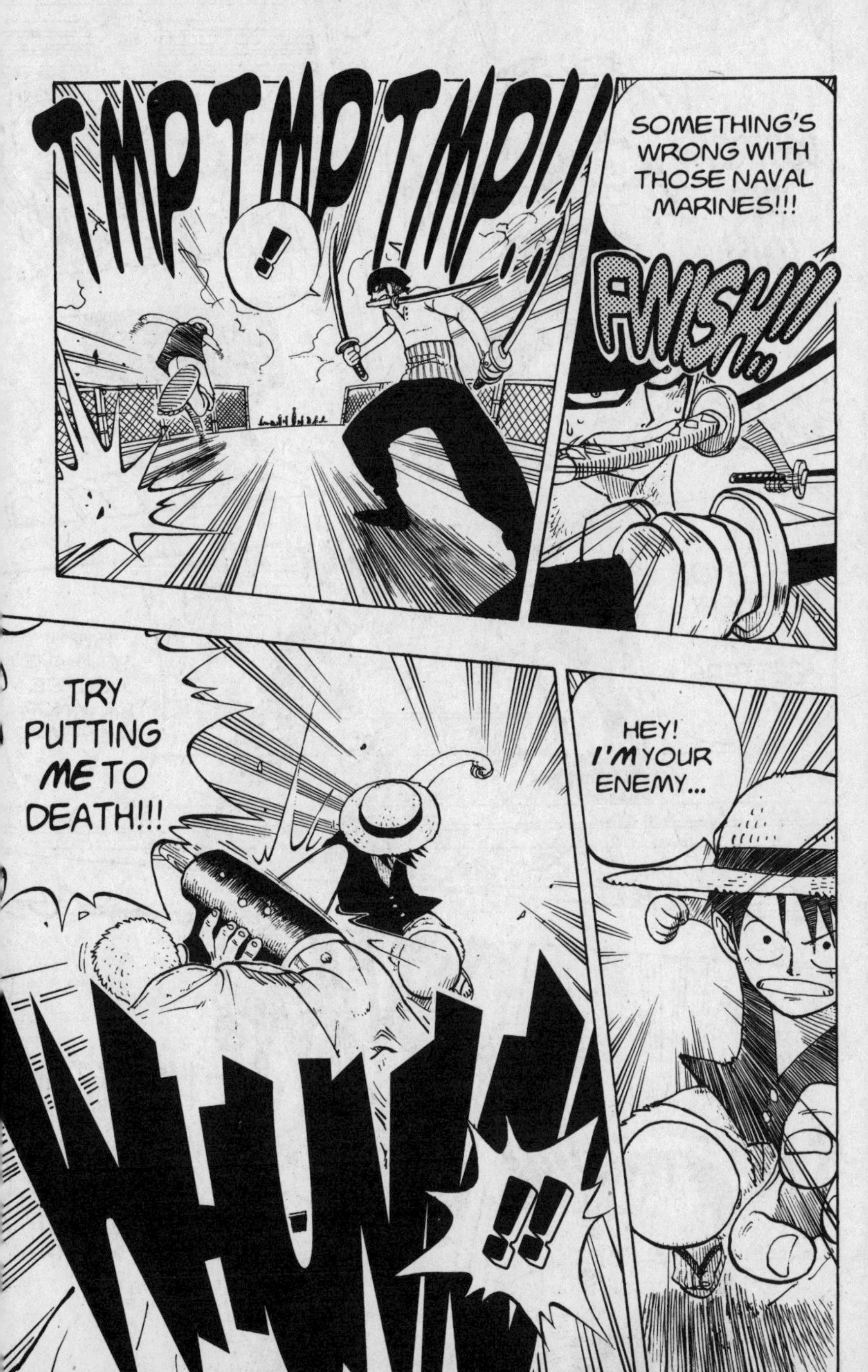
SOMETHING'S WRONG WITH THOSE NAVAL MARINES!!!
FWISH!!
TMP TMP TMP!!
!
HEY! *I'M* YOUR ENEMY...
TRY PUTTING *ME* TO DEATH!!!
THWUNK!!

...!
LUFFY!!!!
DESTROY THIS LOUSY NAVY!!!
HMPH! YOU HAVE NEITHER RANK NOR STATUS!
FWSH
I'LL TEACH YOU TO DEFY YOUR BETTERS!
I'M CAPTAIN AXE-HAND MORGAN!!!
ROWR
NICE TO MEET YOU!
I'M STRAW HAT LUFFY!
TA DA!

DIE!!
!
!!!
WOW!
THAT'S SHARP!!

WMP.
FWA
UNGH!
SKKK!!
...!!
TH-THE CAPTAIN...

BOY...
I SENTENCE YOU TO DEATH!
!
FWOOSH

I'M NOT GONNA DIE.
!?
KA
WA
!!!
HE'S JUST TOO STRONG!!
CAPTAIN MORGAN...
HE'S GETTING PUMMELED!!
MARINE

YOU AND YOUR NAVY...
ARE RUINING KOBY'S DREAM!
!!!
GRB
STOP!!
...
I SAID STOP, YOU IDIOT!!

HELMEPPO...!!
HEH HEH HEH!!
ONE FALSE MOVE AND FOUR EYES GETS IT!!!
IF YOU EVEN BLINK, I'LL SHOOT!
HEY, LUFFY!!
DON'T LET THEM WIN BECAUSE OF ME!
LET HIM KILL ME!!
YOU'RE A GOOD GUY, KOBY!

HEY, IDIOT-SON-OF-THE-CAPTAIN! KOBY MEANS IT!

HEY! I TOLD YOU NOT TO MOVE OR I'D SHOOT!

FINE! I'LL JUST SHOOT HIM THEN!

LUFFY!! BEHIND YOU!

YOU'VE ASSAULTED AN OFFICER OF THE NAVY!!!

GUM-GUM...

KLMP

...PISTOL!

DADDY!! KILL HIM!!

!?

OOF!!!
NICE...
MÖWE

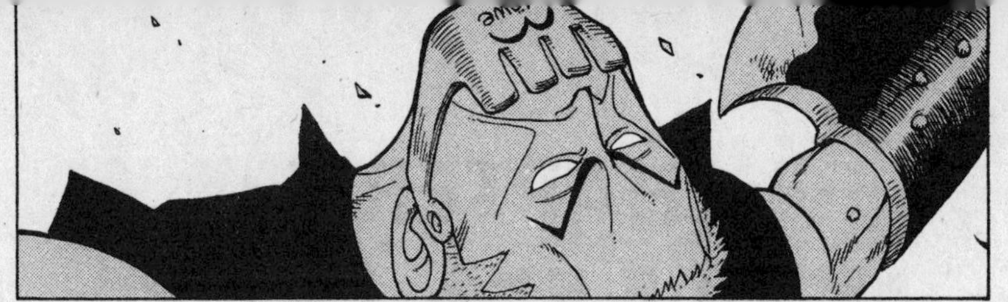

...ZOLO!

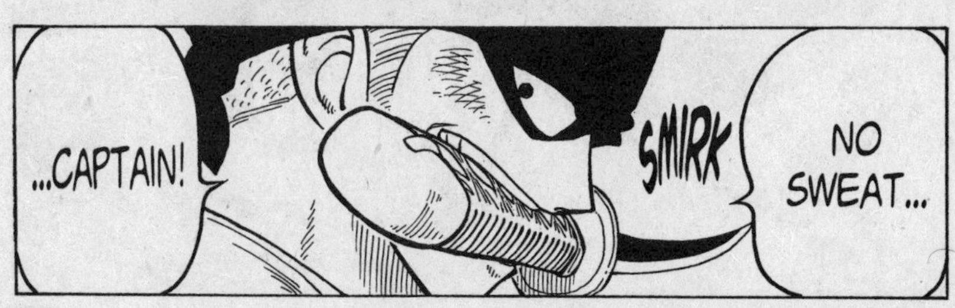
NO SWEAT...
SMIRK
...CAPTAIN!

CHAPTER 7:
FRIENDS

READ THIS WAY

THE CAPTAIN LOST!!!

CAPTAIN MORGAN'S BEEN DEFEATED!!!

TA—DA

CHEEN

ANY OF YOU STILL WANT TO CAPTURE US!?

...?

BANZAI FOR THE NAVY!!
MORGAN'S REIGN OF TERROR IS OVER!!
WE'RE FREE!!
HOORAY!!
YEAAAAAHH!!

THAT MEANS...
...CAPTAIN MORGAN WAS RULING BY FEAR!!

HMPH!
THEY'RE HAPPY WE DEFEATED THEIR CAPTAIN.

ZOLO!?
ZOLO!!

PHEW!
UMPH! I'M STUFFED!!
NOT EATING FOR NINE DAYS WAS WORSE THAN I THOUGHT!!!
STARE
STARE

HA HA HA!
MNCH MNCH

SEE, YOU'D NEVER HAVE SURVIVED THE WHOLE MONTH!
FUNNY... YOU SEEM EVEN HUNGRIER THAN ME!
MNCH MNCH
IT'S KIND OF YOU TO FEED ME ALONG WITH THE HEROES, MA'AM!
IT'S THE LEAST I CAN DO! YOU THREE SAVED THE WHOLE TOWN!!

WOW, YOU'RE GREAT!
YEAH, I'M KINDA GREAT!
TWINKLE
AND I'M GOING TO BECOME A LOT GREATER!

SO...
WHAT'S NEXT?

WE'RE HEADED FOR THE GRAND LINE!

!!!?

THE MOST BLOODTHIRSTY PIRATES IN THE WORLD ARE THERE!!!
HUH!?
THERE ARE ONLY TWO OF YOU! IF YOU GO THERE, YOU'LL JUST BE SAILING TO YOUR DEATHS!
THAT'S SUICIDE!!!

WHAT'S IT TO YOU? YOU'RE NOT COMING WITH US.
ZOLO!? YOU **AGREE** WITH HIM!?
WELL, I GUESS IF WE'RE AFTER THE "**ONE PIECE**"...
...THE GRAND LINE IS WHERE WE HAVE TO GO.

READ THIS WAY

NO, BUT I'M WORRIED ABOUT YOU!
BAMSLAM
CAN'T I WORRY ABOUT... MY FRIENDS?
IS THAT SO WRONG!?
THAT'S NOT WHAT I--

LUFFY, WE HAVEN'T KNOWN EACH OTHER FOR VERY LONG, BUT...
...WE'RE FRIENDS, AREN'T WE?
!

WE'RE GOING OUR SEPARATE WAYS...
...BUT WE'LL ALWAYS BE FRIENDS!!

YOU'RE THE FIRST REAL FRIEND I'VE EVER HAD...
NO ONE ELSE EVER STUCK UP FOR ME!

EVEN I WOULDN'T STICK UP FOR ME!

READ THIS WAY

BUT THE TWO OF YOU...
YOU TAUGHT ME TO FIGHT FOR WHAT I BELIEVE IN!!!

THAT'S WHY I'M GOING TO THE GRAND LINE!
MAKES SENSE TO ME.
WAIT! THAT'S NOT WHAT I--
I'M TRYING TO CONVINCE YOU THAT IT'S TOO RECKLESS!!

WHAT ABOUT ***YOUR*** PLANS?
HUH?
HUH?
YOU WERE CABIN BOY ON ALVIDA'S PIRATE SHIP FOR TWO YEARS.
WATCH OUT FOR THE NAVY'S INTELLIGENCE.
IF THEY FIND OUT ABOUT YOUR BACKGROUND, THEY WON'T LET YOU ENLIST.

EXCUSE ME...

K-REEK!!

!

YOU GENTLEMEN ARE PIRATES...
MARINE
...CORRECT?

THAT'S RIGHT. I EVEN HAVE A CREWMAN NOW!
WHICH MAKES ME A GENUINE PIRATE CAPTAIN!

UM... YOU SAVED OUR BASE AND THIS TOWN...
...AND WE ARE TRULY GRATEFUL TO YOU.
MAR
HOWEVER. WE'RE STILL NAVAL MARINES...
...AND WE CAN'T SHELTER PIRATES.

I'M SORRY, BUT I HAVE TO ASK YOU TO LEAVE.
BUT TO SHOW OUR GRATITUDE, WE WON'T REPORT YOU TO THE NAVY.
NAVY PIGS! WHAT ARE YOU DOING!?
YOU HATED MORGAN AS MUCH AS WE DID!!!
GRR GRR
THEY'RE YOUR SAVIORS, TOO!

I GUESS WE'LL BE GOING, THEN...
MA'AM, THANKS FOR THE MEAL...
...
LUFFY...
YOU'RE LEAVING ALREADY?

!
!
WSH...

...!!

I'M...

AREN'T YOU GOING WITH THEM?
HUH?
I'M...

WE'RE GOING OUR SEPARATE WAYS, BUT WE'LL ALWAYS BE FRIENDS!

I...
I'M NOT ONE OF THEM!!!

...!
EXCUSE ME, PIRATES?

IS THAT TRUE?

...

LET ME EXPLAIN.
I KNOW ALL ABOUT HIS PAST...

!
LUFFY!?
YOU'RE NOT GOING TO...
GASP!

SEE, THERE WAS THIS SECRET ISLAND...
AND A BIG PIRATE WOMAN...
...HER NAME WAS ALVIDA...

GASP!
IF THEY FIND OUT ABOUT YOUR BACKGROUND, THEY WON'T LET YOU ENLIST...
LUFFY, DON'T...

SHE WAS REALLY MEAN...

AND FOR TWO YEARS, THIS GUY...

...

LUFFY!! DON'T!!

SHUT UP!!!

!!?

...!!

...

HUF
HUF
...!!!

WHAM!!

WHY, YOU--!!

STOP DISTURBING THE PEACE!!
ENOUGH!

!
TAKE THAT!
FWAK THWAK
AND THIS!!
BAM

HEY, HEY...
RSSK
THAT'S ENOUGH.

IT'S CLEAR THAT YOU'RE NOT FRIENDS!!!
PLEASE, LEAVE TOWN! NOW!!!
MARINE

WAS THAT HIS PLAN!?
DID HE GOAD ME INTO HITTING HIM!?
...!!!

HE DID IT AGAIN!! IN THE END...
SWSH
CATCH US IF YOU CAN!
SWSH
GASP!
...I STILL DEPEND ON HIS HELP!!!

WHAT AM I...
HELPLESS!?

FWIP
IF I DON'T DEPEND ON MYSELF FROM NOW ON, THEN I AM A LOSER!!!

PLEASE LET ME JOIN THE NAVY, SIR!!!
I'LL BE A CABIN BOY, OR ANYTHING, BUT JUST LET ME JOIN!!!

I'M GONNA DO IT!! I'M GONNA DO IT!!!

LIEUTENANT! I DON'T THINK THAT'S A GOOD IDEA!
I STILL DON'T TRUST HIM!
!
PIRATES HAVE BEEN KNOWN TO PLANT SPIES IN THE NAVY.
WE SHOULD DO A THOROUGH BACK-GROUND CHECK ON HIM.
...

I'M NO PIRATE!!

I'M GONNA BE A NAVY OFFICER!!!

...

MANY OF MY FELLOW SAILORS HAVE BEEN KILLED BY PIRATES...
DON'T TAKE BEING A SAILOR LIGHTLY.
TP TP
YOU'RE ACCEPTED...
YES SIR!
THANK YOU VERY MUCH, SIR!!

READ THIS WAY

THAT WAS SOME PRETTY BAD ACTING...
I WOULDN'T BE SURPRISED IF THEY SAW THROUGH IT.
IT'S ALL UP TO KOBY, NOW. HE'LL GET IN SOMEHOW!

WELL, IT'S A GOOD TIME TO BE LEAVING...
EVERYBODY HATES US... THAT'S THE WAY PIRATES SHOULD LEAVE A TOWN...
HAHAHA. I GUESS THAT'S TRUE!

L-LU--
L-LU--
MARINE
LUFFY!!!
KOBY!

READ
THIS
WAY

THANK YOU VERY MUCH, CAP'N LUFFY!
FWIP!!
I'LL NEVER FORGET ALL YOU DID FOR ME!!!

THIS IS A NEW ONE. A PIRATE BEING SALUTED BY THE NAVY!
HA HA HA!

WE'LL MEET AGAIN, KOBY!!

MARINE
'TEN-SHUN!

FWIP!!
HUH!?

HOORAY!!

YOU'VE GOT SOME GOOD FRIENDS, SAILOR.
!
YES, SIR.
NOW, IT'S AGAINST REGULATIONS TO SALUTE PIRATES LIKE WE JUST DID.
FWIP!
AS PUNISHMENT, WE WON'T GET ANY DINNER FOR ONE WEEK!
YES, SIR!

WE'RE ON OUR WAY!
TO THE GRAND LINE!!!
LUFFY AND HIS FIRST CREWMAN (THE FORMER, INFAMOUS, DEMONIC PIRATE HUNTER ZOLO) SET SAIL...
...NEITHER OF THEM REALIZING THAT THEY'VE MADE ONE SERIOUS MISTAKE...

The Great Age of Piracy

It was an age burning with the magnificence of those searching for the treasure of treasures: "One Piece," hidden by Gold Roger, history's only "King of the Pirates." It was an age when pirates beyond number raised their flags to battle for fame and fortune.

It was a Golden Age...

CHAPTER 8 : NAMI

READ
THIS
WAY

I'M STARVING!
...

DON'T YOU THINK IT'S STRANGE THAT YOU CAN'T NAVIGATE?
NO, DRIFTING HAS WORKED PRETTY WELL FOR ME.

WHAT ABOUT YOU? YOU'RE SUPPOSED TO BE THE HOLY TERROR OF THE SEAS!
I DON'T RECALL EVER CALLING MYSELF THAT.

I FOLLOWED A PIRATE I WAS AFTER OUT TO SEA.
BUT I COULDN'T FIND MY WAY BACK TO MY VILLAGE.

READ THIS WAY

I HAD TO EARN MONEY SOMEHOW...
SO I MADE THE BEST OF THINGS. I WENT AFTER PIRATES THAT WERE IN THE AREA.

HMPH! SO YOU GOT LOST?
YOU DON'T HAVE TO PUT IT LIKE THAT!

ANYWAY, WHAT KIND OF A PIRATE DOESN'T KNOW HOW TO NAVIGATE A SHIP? IT'S RIDICULOUS!
AT THIS RATE, WE'LL NEVER MAKE IT TO THE GRAND LINE.
WE'VE GOT TO RECRUIT A NAVIGATOR AS SOON AS POSSIBLE.

AND WE NEED A COOK, AND A MUSICIAN, AND--
THOSE CAN WAIT!!

FLOP
I'M STARVING!
FLOP

READ THIS WAY

HEY...
IT'S A BIRD...
FWAP
IT LOOKS PRETTY BIG...

FWAP
FWAP

LET'S EAT IT!!
HUH? HOW?
FWIP

LEAVE IT TO ME! I'LL CATCH IT!!
GUM-GUM...
VREEENG

FWAP
FWAP
...ROCKET!!!
BWOING!!

READ THIS WAY

OKAY...

CHOMP
GASP!
WHAT!?

AAAAH!
FWAP
AAAAAH
FWAP
HELP!!
YOU IDIOT!!!

AAAAAH
KREEK
WHAT ARE YOU DOING!?
DAMN YOU!
KREEK
KREEK

READ THIS WAY

KREEK
KREEK
AAAA
HUH!?
IT'S A SHIP! HEY, WAIT!
AHOY!
SHIPWRECK SURVIVORS? AT A TIME LIKE THIS?

I CAN'T STOP! JUST GRAB ON AND CLIMB IN!

HEY!!
SPLASH SPLAP
WHAT'D HE SAY!?

UMF!
SPLAP
WHOA!
WAP

READ THIS WAY

YOU MADE IT! GOOD!
KREEK
YOU WOULD HAVE LEFT US TO DIE!!
KREEK

HUF HUF...
WHAT KIND OF PERSON ARE YOU!!

HEY!
STOP THE SHIP!
FWIP
WE'RE PIRATES OF BUGGY THE CLOWN!

HUH!?

READ THIS WAY

KREEK KREEK
HEE HEE HEE...
STROKE!
STROKE!
WE'RE SORRY, MR. PIRATE HUNTER ZOLO, SIR! WE DIDN'T REALIZE WHO YOU WERE!!

YOU JOKERS MADE ME LOSE MY FRIEND!
KREEK
KREEK
KEEP ROWING. IF THERE'S ANY LAND NEARBY, HE'LL GET THERE.

SO, HOW DID YOU PIRATES END UP SOAKING IN THE MIDDLE OF THE OCEAN?
I'LL TELL YOU HOW!!! THANKS FOR REMINDING US!

IT WAS THAT WOMAN!!
IT WAS ALL HER FAULT!!!
SHE WAS A REAL LOOKER, THOUGH!!

WE HAD JUST FINISHED RAIDING A MERCHANT SHIP...
...!
HAR HAR HAR HAR!!
THIS IS A PRETTY GOOD HAUL!
NOT A BAD, FOR A SMALL SHIP!
MAYBE CAPTAIN BUGGY WILL GIVE US A REWARD!
HUH?
A BOAT!
THERE'S A BODY IN IT.

HEY... A GIRL!
WHAT'S WRONG, GIRL? HAR HAR HAR! ARE YOU DEAD?
OH... I'M SEEING THINGS...
...THERE CAN'T BE ANYONE HERE IN THE VAST SEA...
I DON'T KNOW WHO YOU ARE...
...BUT COULD YOU SPARE A LITTLE WATER?
AND MAYBE A PIECE OF BREAD?
I'M LOST AT SEA!
BUT PLEASE... HELP ME.
SURE, WE'LL HELP YOU...
BUT FIRST LET'S JUST TAKE A PEEK IN THAT TREASURE CHEST!
PANT
PANT

GO AHEAD, TAKE WHATEVER YOU WANT...
BUT PLEASE... SOME WATER!?
PATIENCE LITTLE LADY! FIRST, WE GOTTA SEE YOUR TREASURE!
HAR HAR
KLOMP
AFTER ALL, WE'RE SAVING YOUR LIFE!

TAKE THE WHOLE SHIP!
HEE HEE
IT'S ALL YOURS!

HEY!!
SHE'S LEAVING WITH OUR SHIP... AND OUR TREASURE!!
HEY! THIS CHEST IS EMPTY!!!

DARK CLOUDS COMING IN LOW FROM THE SOUTH...
SHAOOOO
!?
THAT MEANS A COLD FRONT, FOLKS...
WITH A STRONG LIKELI-HOOD OF VIOLENT SHOWERS...
THERE'S A SQUALL LINE HEADING THIS WAY...
SMALL VESSELS SHOULD TAKE PRECAUTIONS AGAINST CAPSIZING.

BINGO!
ARRGH!!!
KRAKK!!!!

THWAP
SO LONG! AND THANKS FOR THE TREASURE!

S-SHE TRICKED US!!!
KSSSH
WE'LL GET YOU FOR THIS!

...AND THAT'S THE WHOLE SAD STORY!
JUST AWFUL, AIN'T IT!?
AMAZING. SHE USED THE WEATHER TO HER OWN ADVANTAGE. SHE MUST REALLY KNOW THE SEAS...
SHE'D MAKE A GREAT NAVI-GATOR...

WE THINK SHE'LL MAKE A GREAT CORPSE!
WHAT'LL WE DO ABOUT THE TREASURE WE LOST?
IF WE RETURN EMPTY-HANDED, BUGGY WILL BE FURIOUS!
WHO'S THIS BUGGY GUY ANYWAY?

ONLY THE MOST FERO-CIOUS PIRATE IN THESE PARTS!
HAVEN'T YOU HEARD OF BUGGY THE CLOWN? HE ATE THE **FRUIT OF THE DEVIL!**
...THE FRUIT OF THE DEVIL?

DA DUM

READ THIS WAY

STOP, THIEF!!
GIVE US BACK THAT MAP!
TATATATAT
HUF
HUF
TATATATAT
I FINALLY HAVE IT!
KRCH
A MAP OF THE ***GRAND LINE!!***

I DON'T WANT TO BE KILLED BY ONE OF THE CAPTAIN'S CANNON-BALLS!
IF WE DON'T GET THAT MAP BACK, WE'RE DEAD!
KLOMP
KLOMP
KLOMP
KLOMP
CAP'N BUGGY! THERE'S SOMETHING ODD IN THE SKY!
SHOOT IT DOWN WITH THE CANNON!
AAAAAAA
AYE AYE, SIR!

HEY!
!!?
!?
AAAHH!
EEEYAA!
I-IT'S A KID!
HE FELL FROM THE SKY!!!
WHAT!?
WHO'S SHOOTING CANNON-BALLS AT ME!?
FSS
OUCH!
FSS

DA DA

HE'S NOT HURT!!!

PHEW!

I'M ALIVE!

?!

!
...

YOU CAME TO RESCUE ME!
BOSS!

I'LL JUST LET YOU TAKE CARE OF THOSE GUYS!
ZIP!
HEY! SHE'S GETTING AWAY!
FORGET THE GIRL!

WE'VE GOT HER BOSS RIGHT HERE!
DOOM
HE'S A BIGGER PRIZE THAN SHE IS!
Hanswurst
?

ISN'T THAT RIGHT... BOSS!?
THAT MAP BELONGS TO THE FEARSOME PIRATE, BUGGY THE CLOWN!!!
WAP!
HEY...
CHUNK
!!!
HEY!
KRSSH!
DON'T TOUCH...
...THE HAT!
PTT

WHY YOU...
...SCURVY BILGE-RAT!!

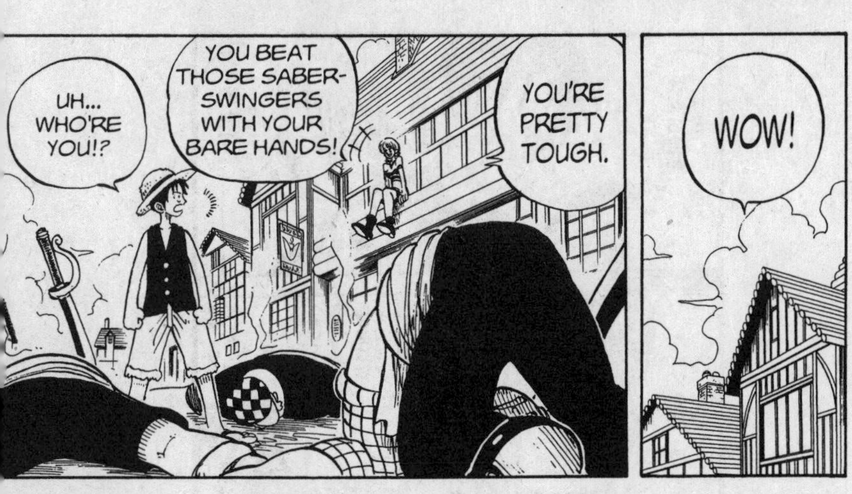
WOW!
YOU'RE PRETTY TOUGH.
YOU BEAT THOSE SABER-SWINGERS WITH YOUR BARE HANDS!
UH... WHO'RE YOU!?

THE NAME'S NAMI!! I SPECIALIZE IN ROBBING PIRATES.

WANNA TEAM UP WITH ME!?

ROBBING PIRATES?

THE MAKING OF ONE PIECE

Before creating the final version of **One Piece** printed in this graphic novel, Eiichiro Oda drew two early one-shot stories starring Luffy, under the title **Romance Dawn** (the same title used for chapter 1 of the final version). These stories aren't part of the plot of **One Piece**—they're like "alternate universe" versions telling a similar story of Luffy's origin. Here's a page from each of the untranslated early versions.

お前宝物はあるか？
宝物？
……この帽子さ
オレの宝物だけど
オレのじゃないんだ
昔オレの住んでた町を一時期拠点にしてたピースメインがいて
はははルフィ!!
お前なんかが海賊になれるか!!
カ・ナ・ヅ・チは海賊にとって致命的だぜ!!
はっはっはっはっはっ
船から落ちなきゃいいだろ
それにそのうち泳げる様になる
つれてってくれよ次の航海!!
ああいいともあと10歳年とったらな
ケチ!!
ルフィ!!海賊は楽しいぜェ
海は広いし大きいし!!いろんな島を冒険するんだ
何より自由っ!!

ROMANCE DAWN: VERSION 1

Drawn about a year and a half before **One Piece** began, this version was printed in one of the **Shonen Jump Specials** showcasing upcoming artists. In it, Luffy fights a pirate named Jolly of the Crescent Moon. Luffy's origin is the same as in **One Piece**—he gets his treasured straw hat from his idol, Shanks.

それは魔性の木の実
なんだぞっ!!!
!
食えば一生泳げない体に
なっちまうんだア!!!
えーーーっ!!
うそーーーっ!!!
バカモンがアーーっ!!!
本当に一生泳げねェんだ……
まーいいや どうせ海賊になりたい訳じゃないんだし
なんだ
ちっ
今まで通りおよげねーだけだ
立ち直りの早いガキめ! おもしろーないわい
まア!! お前が海を嫌っておったのがせめてもの救いだな!!
ぶわっはっはっはっは
大丈夫だ!! 水に携わらず楽しくやっとる人間などいくらでもおるわ!!
!
グイッ

ROMANCE DAWN: VERSION 2

Now the art is more like **One Piece**. Printed as a one-shot in **Weekly Shonen Jump** itself, this version changes Luffy's origin: he gets the Gum-Gum Fruit, and his straw hat, from his grandfather. Oda's explanation: "I didn't want the readers of **Weekly Shonen Jump** to find out about the existence of Shanks because when serialization started, it would lose its impact. Yes, I am a cheeky new artist." In it, Luffy fights a pirate captain who uses magic, a plot element absent from **One Piece** itself.

FACTS ABOUT EIICHIRO ODA

Creator, Artist and Author of **One Piece**

Birthdate:
January 1, 1975
Greek Astrological Sign:
Capricorn
Chinese Astrological Sign:
Rabbit
Blood Type:
A
Favorite Animals:
Big, gentle dogs
Favorite Video Game:
Puyo Puyo
Favorite Music:
'70s soul music
Hidden Talent:
Makes good coffee
Places He's Been:
Japan, America
Favorite Real-Life Pirate:
Blackbeard (Edward Teach)
Interesting Possessions:
Legos, Playmobils, figures, swords, flintlocks, a cow skull

"Most congenial of innkeepers,
Your customer has entered.
Where would you like me to sit?
Those who must sit by the entrance
Cannot be at ease."

It's got a nice ring to it, doesn't it?
A song from the pirates of northern Europe.

–Eiichiro Oda, 1998

CA SIVE IN
OVA. Ao 1492 a Christophoro
nomine regis Castellæ primum detecta.
Noua
Fran
cia.
Chilaga
Calicuas
Tagil.
Flori
da.
Marata
Hispania
Caribana
CTIALIS
Pe ru.
AR DEL ZVR.
Insulæ
incognita
CVS CAPRICORNI
EL MAR
PACIFICO.
Archipelago
de las islas

ONE PIECE

Vol. 2

BUGGY THE CLOWN

STORY AND ART BY

EIICHIRO ODA

Monkey D. Luffy
He ate the fruit of the Gum-Gum Tree, gaining stretchy powers. He wants to become King of the Pirates—and find his hero, "Red-Haired" Shanks.

"Red-Haired" Shanks
A pirate captain. He saved young Luffy's life, losing his arm in the battle, and taught Luffy a love of the sea.

THE STORY OF ONE PIECE

· VOLUME 2 ·

It is the Golden Age of Piracy. Countless pirates sail the seas, searching for legendary pirate Gold Roger's mysterious treasure, the "One Piece." Among them is Monkey D. Luffy, who grew up listening to the wild tales of buccaneer "Red-Haired" Shanks and dreaming of becoming a pirate himself. Having eaten the fruit of the Gum-Gum Tree, Luffy has the bizarre power to stretch like rubber—at the cost of being unable to swim!

Buggy's Pirate Crew
Mohji, Buggy and Cabaji.

Roronoa Zolo
Although he's won fame as a pirate hunter, his true dream is to become the world's greatest swordsman.

Now Luffy's quest to become King of the Pirates has begun. He's found an unlikely friend and crewmate in the fearsome pirate hunter Zolo. But Luffy and Zolo are separated and run afoul of the ruthless pirate Captain Buggy and his gang. Meanwhile, Luffy meets Nami the thief, who specializes in robbing pirates. With an untrustworthy thief at his side and enraged pirates on his tail, Luffy's career on the high seas is already in big trouble. And he's about to learn the terrible secret of Captain Buggy's success.

Nami
A freelance thief who targets pirates for her robberies.

ONE PIECE
ONE PIECE

Vol. 2
BUGGY THE CLOWN

CONTENTS

Chapter 9: FEMME FATALE

READ
THIS
WAY

THAT'S RIGHT!

I STEAL TREASURE FROM PIRATES!

TOGETHER WE COULD MAKE A FORTUNE!

NAMI THE PIRATE ROBBER

I DON'T WANT TO TEAM UP WITH YOU.

HEY, WAIT A MINUTE!

SPROING

TMP

TMP

READ THIS WAY

WHY'D YOU GET SO MAD WHEN THAT GUY TOUCHED YOUR HAT?
IS IT VALUABLE?
THIS HAT IS MY TREASURE.

TREASURE, HUH? DO YOU KEEP JEWELS HIDDEN IN IT?
OR A TREASURE MAP!?
AWW, LEAVE ME ALONE. I'VE GOT THINGS TO DO.

ON THE ROOF OF A TAVERN...
WHAK
BOOM
BANG
KRASH

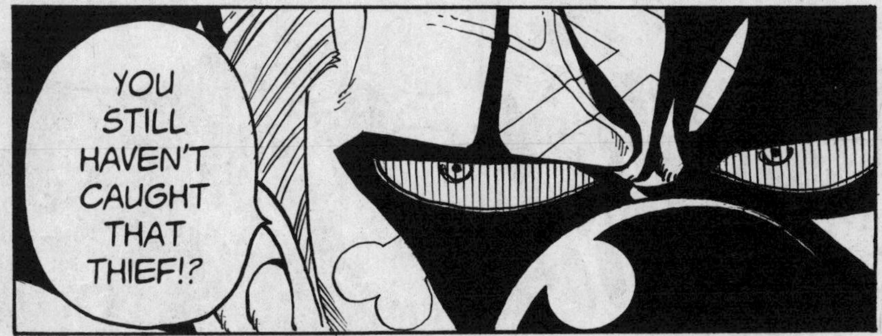
YOU STILL HAVEN'T CAUGHT THAT THIEF!?

READ THIS WAY

W-WE'RE STILL SEARCHING FOR HER, CAPTAIN BUGGY...

THIS IS INEXCUSABLE!!
HOW COULD YOU LET THE MAP OF THE GRAND LINE GET STOLEN!?

AND JUST WHEN WE WERE ABOUT TO HEAD THERE...
...AND RAISE SOME HELL!!!

WELL YOU SEE, CAP'N, SIR... SOMEHOW, THE KEY TO THE MAP ROOM GOT LEFT IN THE LOCK...
AND ONLY THE ROBBER KNOWS--
WHAT DID YOU SAY!?

I SAID, ROBBER KNOWS--
WHAT? RUBBER NOSE??
YIKES!
KRASH!!

READ THIS WAY

DOES MY NOSE LOOK FUNNY TO YOU? YOU THINK IT LOOKS FAKE?
NO, NO... IT'S A MISTAKE! I MEANT THE THIEF!
GRRRRRR
GULP
ULP

SO NOW IT'S A STEAK?! IT LOOKS LIKE BEEF?!!
BUT...
FOR THIS YOU DIE!!!
CAP'N, WAIT!! I NEVER SAID--

WHO AM I?

UMF!!
I CAN'T BREATHE! C-CAPTAIN... BUGGY...
WHOMP

!!!
BUG... UG... UGH... UG...
FWUMP
KLOMP
KLOMP

HE'S USING THE POWER!
GASP!
...OF THE FRUIT OF THE DEVIL!!
READY CANNON...
PIRATE CAPTAIN BUGGY THE CLOWN

AAAAAAAA!

KOFF KOFF
I... NEVER... SP-SPARE ME!
BLAST HIM TO PIECES!

KABOOOM
AAAAAAAAA
AND GET ME MY MAP!!
AND TAKE EVERYTHING OF VALUE FROM THIS TOWN!!
STP
STP

AYE AYE, CAP'N!
CAPTAIN BUGGY, SIR!

READ THIS WAY

WEIRD...
SO YOU LOST YOUR CREW AT SEA?
HOW BIG IS YOUR CREW?

JUST ONE OTHER GUY. IS THIS YOUR HOUSE?
NO. MY WORK KEEPS ME ON THE MOVE. I DON'T KNOW WHOSE HOUSE IT IS.
THE TOWN IS PRACTICALLY DESERTED.
EVERYONE WANTS TO STAY AS FAR FROM THE TAVERN AS POSSIBLE. THAT'S WHERE BUGGY AND HIS PIRATES ARE.

BUGGY...
...THE INFAMOUS, CANNON-HAPPY BUCCANEER.
HMMM...
ARE NAMI AND HIS MEN REALLY THAT SCARY?
I'M NAMI!
BUGGY IS THE PIRATE!!!
DON'T MIX ME UP WITH HIM!

READ THIS WAY

THEY SAY SOME KIDS IN A VILLAGE MADE FUN OF HIS NOSE.
BUGGY'S CANNONS BLEW THE VILLAGE TO SMITHEREENS...
AND WHAT'S MORE...
I'VE HEARD THAT BUGGY HAS MYSTERIOUS POWERS.

HMMM... I WONDER WHY THERE'S NO ONE AROUND HERE...
I TOLD YOU! EVERYBODY RAN AWAY 'CAUSE THEY'RE SCARED OF BUGGY!!

OH! SO YOU'RE LOOTING THE ABANDONED HOUSES?
OF COURSE NOT! I ROB PIRATES, NOT VILLAGERS!!
WOMP!!

I'M NOT SOME LOW-DOWN LOOTER!!
YOU'RE GIVING ME A HEADACHE!
TAKE IT EASY!
HA HA HA

SIGH
...

I'VE GOT TO GET A HUNDRED MILLION BERRIES!!
THEN I'M GOING TO BUY A CERTAIN VILLAGE!!

BUY A VILLAGE?
FOR A HUNDRED MILLION BERRIES? THAT'S A LOT OF MONEY, EVEN FOR A GREAT PIRATE...
I'VE GOT A PLAN...

SEE THIS?
I JUST STOLE IT. IT'S A MAP OF THE GRAND LINE!
TA
DA

AFTER I STEAL BUGGY THE CLOWN'S TREASURE...
...I'M GOING TO HEAD FOR THE GRAND LINE...

AND THEN I'LL STEAL THE TREASURES OF EVEN BIGGER PIRATES!!

READ THIS WAY

WHAT DO YOU THINK?
TEAM UP WITH ME, AND YOU'LL MAKE A FORTUNE!
I COULD USE A TOUGH GUY LIKE YOU.
WE'LL SPLIT THE LOOT, 50-50!

HEY!
DO YOU KNOW ANYTHING ABOUT NAVI-GATING?
WHAT?

OF COURSE I DO!
I'M THE BEST NAVIGATOR AROUND!
I LOVE THE SEA!

WOW! THAT'S GREAT!
WE'RE HEADED FOR THE GRAND LINE TOO!!

READ THIS WAY

REALLY!?

YEAH! AND YOU COULD BE OUR NAVI-GATOR!!
WILL YOU JOIN MY PIRATE CREW!
!

!!
NO WAY!!!
?

HMPH...
I DIDN'T KNOW THAT YOU WERE A PIRATE!
FORGET EVERY-THING I SAID! I'D NEVER TEAM UP WITH YOU!

READ THIS WAY

I GET IT... YOU'RE AFTER SOME FANTASTIC TREASURE AND YOU KEEP THE MAP IN THAT HAT OF YOURS.

I TOLD YOU, THERE'S NO MAP IN MY HAT!
THEN WHY IS THAT RAGGEDY OLD HAT SO PRECIOUS TO YOU, LIAR?

I TREASURE THIS HAT BECAUSE A FRIEND GAVE IT TO ME A LONG TIME AGO.
THAT'S WHEN I SWORE I'D GATHER A CREW AND BECOME A PIRATE.

HMPH! PIRATES, PHOOEY!
THESE ARE CRAZY TIMES.

IF THERE'S ONE THING IN THIS WORLD I REALLY HATE...
...IT'S PIRATES!!
BUT I LOVE MONEY! AND TANGERINES!

THIS GUY'S A STUPID, WORTHLESS PLUNDERER...
HE DOESN'T SEEM TO HAVE ANYTHING WORTH STEALING... BUT MAYBE HE COULD STILL BE OF USE TO ME...

SO HOW 'BOUT IT? WANNA BE MY NAVIGATOR?
I TOLD YOU TO FORGET ABOUT IT!
YOU NO-GOOD PIRATE!!
I GOT IT!
SMIRK

READ THIS WAY

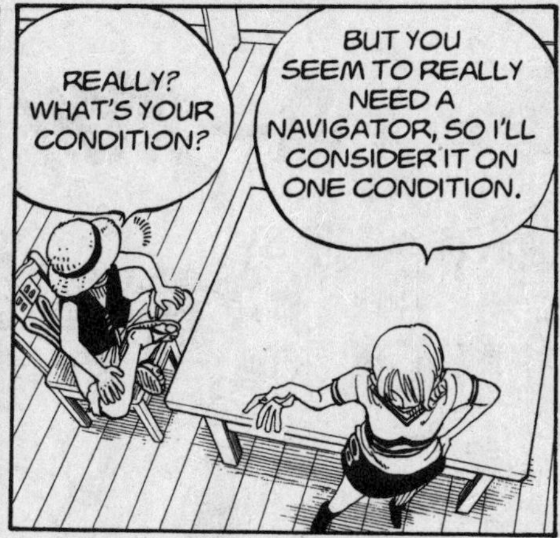
BUT YOU SEEM TO REALLY NEED A NAVIGATOR, SO I'LL CONSIDER IT ON ONE CONDITION.
REALLY? WHAT'S YOUR CONDITION?

JUST A LITTLE THING. IT'S NOTHING, REALLY.
GO WITH ME TO SEE BUGGY.

YOU GOT IT! LET'S GO!
WHERE IS THIS BUGGY?
KLAK
KLAK
HOLD ON, I HAVE TO GET READY.

WHAT'S THAT ROPE FOR?
OH, I ALWAYS CARRY A ROPE.

SO, YOU WANT TO BE A PIRATE, DO YOU?

READ THIS WAY

IT'S JUST AT THE END OF THIS STREET.

THAT'S THE TAVERN WHERE THE PIRATES HANG OUT.
DA—DOOM
SO, WHAT ARE WE GOING TO DO THERE?

WELL...
FWP
HUH?
...
YOU'LL SEE...
...WHEN WE GET THERE...
MR. PIRATE-BREECHES!
SQUEEZE!!
WHAT'RE YOU DOING!?
FWUMP!!

READ THIS WAY

WHAT!?
YOU LET THAT THIEF GET AWAY!?
YOU'RE TELLING ME A LITTLE TART OUTRAN THREE OF MY BEST MEN!?

A THOUSAND PARDONS, CAP'N BUGGY!
BUT HER BOSS, THE GUY IN THE STRAW HAT, WAS REALLY STRONG!

FOR THIS YOU DIE!!
GULP!!!
AAAAAH!!!

READ THIS WAY

CAP'N BUGGY!!
EH!?
WHAT IS IT!?

IT'S THE MAP-STEALER...
SHE JUST WALKED IN THE DOOR...

GOOD! BRING HER HERE!!

I MEAN... BELAY THAT! WHAT'S HER GAME!?
WHY'D SHE COME BACK!?
HMM...
BEATS ME, BUT SHE'S HERE.
VERY WELL! BRING HER TO ME!

C-CAP'N BUGGY! IT'S HIM! SHE'S WITH HIM!
HE'S THE GUY WHO FELL OUT OF THE SKY!!

SPLUMP!!
OOF!

CAPTAIN BUGGY! I'VE CAPTURED THE THIEF!
!
AND HERE'S YOUR MAP!
...

HEY! YOU TRICKED ME!
HMM... YOU'RE RETURNING THE MAP?
WHAT'S ALL THIS ABOUT?

I HAD A DISPUTE WITH MY EMPLOYER!
HE'S AN IDIOT, SO I THOUGHT I'D JOIN UP WITH YOU!

HUH?
...
HA HA HA HA HA HA HA HA HA HA HA!!
HA HA HA HA HA HA HA HA HA HA!!
IDIOT, EH? YOU'VE GOT SPUNK! I THINK I WILL LET YOU JOIN MY CREW!

INFILTRATION ACCOMPLISHED! NOW TO GRAB BUGGY'S TREASURE AND THE MAP OF THE GRAND LINE...
...AND MAKE A QUICK GETAWAY!!
JUST FORGET ABOUT JOINING MY CREW, NOW!
KLANG!!!

HEH HEHHEH
THIS IS IT, MASTER ZOLO.

IT LOOKS LIKE A GHOST TOWN.
WHERE IS EVERYONE?
...

WELL YOU SEE, SIR... WE'VE TAKEN OVER THE TOWN.
WHAT'LL WE TELL CAPTAIN BUGGY?
WE'RE COMING BACK EMPTY-HANDED...
WE'LL JUST HAVE TO TELL HIM THE TRUTH. IT'S ALL THAT GIRL'S FAULT!

C'MON. TAKE ME TO YOUR CAPTAIN.

MAYBE HE KNOWS WHERE LUFFY IS.

BA-DOOM!!

One Piece Rough Sketch!

吹き飛ばせ
バギー海賊団船長
"道化のバギー"
やめてくれ おれは何も言ってねェ!!
コソ泥はまだ捕まらねェのか!?
ズドォン
ギャアアア
ま…まだ追跡中のようで…
大砲をブッ放せ!! ハデにな!!

Chapter 10:
INCIDENT AT THE TAVERN

READ THIS WAY

AT THE TAVERN, "THE DRINKER PUB"...
THE MAP OF THE GRAND LINE IS MINE AGAIN!
AND WE HAVE A NEW CREWMATE!! EVERYTHING IS GOING OUR WAY!!

DA-DUM
EVERYBODY RAISE A GLASS!
LIVE IT UP, MEN! HERE'S TO OUR NEXT CONQUEST!

HOORAY!!!...
ARRR!

READ THIS WAY

NAMI!! ARE YOU KNOCKIN' EM BACK!?
ARR!
AYE AYE, CAP'N BUGGY!!

TIME FOR A DRINKING CONTEST, NEW GIRL!!
GLUG GLUG GLUG
YOU'RE ON!!

I WIN!
!!
WOW

HEH HEH... NOBODY CAN OUT-DRINK ME! AT THIS RATE THEY'LL ALL PASS OUT SOON.
THEN THEIR TREASURE WILL BE ALL MINE! PIRATES ARE SUCH EASY PREY!

READ THIS WAY

CHANG
CHOMP!
CHANG
CHOMP!
CHANG

LOOKS LIKE THEY'RE HAVING FUN.
THAT'S WHAT A PIRATE'S SUPPOSED TO DO!

GRR!

HOW YA DOIN', "BOSS?"
LET ME OUTTA HERE!
AND GET ME SOME-THING TO EAT!
I'M STARVING!

READ THIS WAY

MM MM!
HA HA HA
MNCH MNCH
YOU'RE NOT SO BAD. MAYBE I'LL LET YOU JOIN MY CREW AFTER ALL!
NEVER!!

DON'T YOU REALIZE WHAT'S GOING TO HAPPEN TO YOU?
THEY'LL PROBABLY SELL YOU OFF SOMEWHERE.

BUT HEY, IF MY PLAN WORKS...
MAYBE I'LL GIVE YOU THE KEY TO THIS CAGE.
REALLY, YOU DON'T SEEM SO BAD... FOR A PIRATE.
THEN LET ME OUT OF HERE NOW!

HA HA HA HA HA HA HA HA HA!!!
!!
GASP!
YOU PICKED THE WRONG PARTNER, LITTLE THIEF!!

READ THIS WAY

PARTNER? SHE'S NOT MY PARTNER!

NOT ANYMORE, EH? CAN'T BLAME YOU!
HEH HEH HEH HEH
SHE BETRAYED YOU, AFTER ALL!?

THE PUNISHMENT FOR TRYING TO STEAL MY TREASURE IS SEVERE!
I'VE ALREADY DECIDED WHAT YOUR FATE SHALL BE.
ARE YOU GONNA LET ME GO?
THAT'S RIGHT, I'M GOING TO LET YOU GO--
OF COURSE I'M NOT GOING TO LET YOU GO!!
ARE YOU DAFT!?

LOAD THE SPECIAL BUGGY BALLS!!

YAAR!

HOORAY!!

READ THIS WAY
PA DUM!
BOOM
BUGGY BALL READY, CAP'N!
VERY WELL!
NOW FOR A DEMON-STRATION... OF POWER!
!!!

BOOOM-UUM-UU
!!?
Drinker
-OOM-OOM-OOM
...
YAAAY!!!
BREATHTAKING! THAT WOULD HAVE LEVELED A SMALLER TOWN!!!
WITH THESE BUGGY BALLS-- AND THE SPECIAL POWERS I GOT FROM EATING THE DEVIL FRUIT--I'LL RULE THE GRAND LINE!!!

READ THIS WAY

DA-DUM!

NOW IT'S YOUR TURN, GIRLIE!!

PROVE YOUR LOYALTY BY BLOWING YOUR FORMER BOSS INTO MINCEMEAT WITH THIS BUGGY BALL!

SHOW ME YOU'RE RUTHLESS ENOUGH TO HELP ME TAKE OVER THE WORLD!

KILL YOUR FORMER BOSS!!!

YOU WANT ME TO...
...K-KILL HIM?

TH-THAT'S OKAY, CAPTAIN BUGGY...
I DON'T NEED TO DO THAT...

HEY, LET'S JUST DRINK SOME MORE INSTEAD!?
LET'S FORGET ABOUT THAT LOSER!!

DO IT.

UM...
YEAAHH!!!!
DO IT! NOW!! BLOW HIM TO PIECES!!
BLAST HIM!! BLAST HIM!

BLOW HIM APART!

ULP!

DO IT!

...!!

BLOW HIM TO PIECES!

BLAST HIM!
YEAH!
DO IT!
YARR!!
BLOW 'IM TO PIECES!!

OH NO... WHAT SHOULD I DO?
IF I DON'T KILL HIM, THEY'LL KILL ME!
ARRR! ARRR!

HE'S JUST A NO-GOOD PIRATE, BUT...
IF I MURDER HIM IN COLD BLOOD, THEN I'LL BE AS BAD AS A PIRATE TOO!

...

NAMI!!! STOP STALLING AND LIGHT THE CANNON!
DO IT! DO IT!

READ THIS WAY
YOUR HANDS ARE SHAKING.
!

THAT'S WHAT YOU GET...
...FOR GOING UP AGAINST PIRATES UNPREPARED!

UNPREPARED!? YOU MEAN NOT BEING PREPARED TO KILL SOMEONE LIKE IT'S NOTHING?
IS THAT WHAT "PREPARED" MEANS TO A PIRATE?
DO IT! DO IT!
NO.

READ THIS WAY

QUIT STALLING!!
IT MEANS BEING PREPARED TO RISK YOUR OWN LIFE!!
BLAST HIM!
AYE!
DO IT!!
ARR!
WHAT'SA MATTER, NEW GIRL!?
DON'T YA KNOW HOW TO FIRE A CANNON?
FSSSK
!
SRRT
IT'S EASY.
JUST PUT THE FLAME TO THE FUSE, AND...
KRAK
KRAK!!

THWACK
!!?
HUH!?
KLINK
!!

HUF HUF...
TRAITOR!! AND AFTER I WELCOMED YOU INTO MY CREW!
DARN! I COULDN'T HELP MYSELF.
I JUST GOT CARRIED AWAY...
I JUST DON'T WANT TO BECOME A LOW-DOWN MURDERER LIKE ALL OF YOU!!
WHOA, ARE YOU GOING TO SAVE ME AFTER ALL?
DON'T BE STUPID!!

YOU PIRATES TOOK SOMEONE DEAR TO ME...

I'LL NEVER BECOME WHAT I HATE!!!

...

OH... SO THAT'S WHY YOU HATE PIRATES.

DA-BOOM!!
YIKES!
THE FUSE IS LIT!!!
FSSSS

UH-OH!!!
CHANG
CHANG
CHANG
I'M GONNA DIE!!!
CHANG

FSSSSS
LITTLE GIRL, YOU TRIED TO MAKE A FOOL OF ME!!
FOR THAT, YOU DIE!!
DIE!!!!....
WHRRRR
AAA
!!
FSSSSS
THE FUSE IS STILL LIT...

READ THIS WAY
CHANG
CHANG
FSSS
DARN! I'LL BE BLOWN TO BITS!!!
CHANG
...
YOU MISSED!!
!!?

FSSSSS
NO WAY! I'LL NEVER GIVE UP!
CHANG
CHANG
CHANG
CHANG
FSSSS
FWP
!!
FSSS...
!
YARR!!
BEHIND YOU!!
HEY! LOOK OUT!!
AGGH...!
NNGH...

BA
HOW MANY PIRATES DOES IT TAKE TO HANDLE ONE GIRL?
!!!?
BAM
!
...?
ZOLO !!!

!
ZOLO!!
WHOA WOW
YOU HURT?
NO, I'M OKAY...
PHEW! I'M GLAD YOU FOUND ME!
NOW GET ME OUTTA HERE!
ALWAYS GOOFING AROUND...
TAP TAP
FIRST YOU FLY OFF WITH A BIRD, AND NOW YOU'RE PLAYING IN SOME CAGE...
FOOL!
HEY, DID HE JUST CALL THAT GUY Z-ZOLO?
WHAT'S ZOLO THE PIRATE HUNTER DOING TALKING TO THAT THIEF?
THE CREWMATE HE WAS TALKING ABOUT...
THAT WAS ZOLO THE PIRATE HUNTER?
WHAT'S GOING ON HERE?

DOOOM
SO YOU'RE RORONOA ZOLO, EH?
YOU MUST HAVE COME TO CAPTURE ME!
I GAVE UP PIRATE HUNTING.
I HAVE NO INTEREST IN YOU.

WELL, I AM INTERESTED IN YOU. KILLING YOU WILL BE A NICE FEATHER IN MY CAP.
FWIP FWIP
BACK OFF BEFORE I PLUCK ALL YOUR FEATHERS.

GET'IM, CAP'N BUGGY! CUT'IM TO PIECES!!
YARR!
GIVE ME ALL YOU'VE GOT, PIRATE HUNTER, 'CAUSE I'M ABOUT TO GET A LOOK AT YOUR BLOOD!!!
YOU ASKED FOR IT!
...!

HEY!
THAT WAS TOO EASY!

NO WAY...

HEH HEH...

VIKINGS, PART 1

- All pirates are sea-roving plunderers, but throughout history there have been many different kinds of pirates in different times and places.

- I want to talk about one of my favorite kinds of pirates: the Vikings.

- Over a thousand years ago, Viking raiders swept down from Scandinavia and ran amok through Europe.

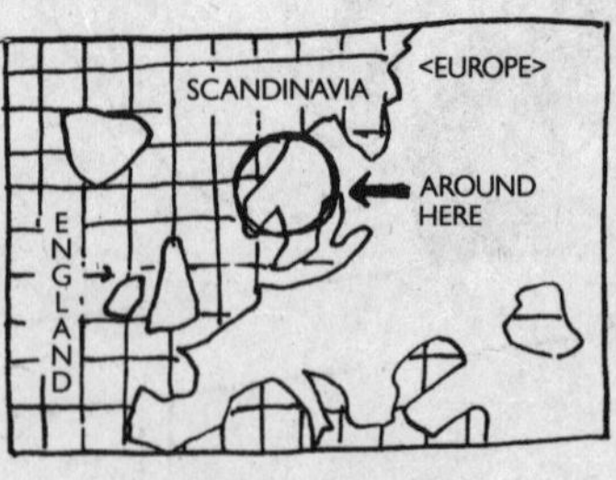
SCANDINAVIA
<EUROPE>
AROUND HERE
ENGLAND

  They came from the present-day countries of Norway, Sweden and Denmark. As to why they were called Vikings, well, that's easy: that's what they called themselves. Why did they call themselves Vikings? To know that, we'd have to go back a thousand years and ask them.

Chapter 11:
FLIGHT

FLUMP!!

FLUMP

HMPH!
THAT WAS ALMOST DISAP-POINTING...

HEH HEH HEH...
...?

READ THIS WAY

HEY ZOLO! GET ME OUTTA HERE!
!
RIGHT...
KLAK

WHAT'S WITH THOSE PIRATES?
THEIR CAPTAIN GETS KILLED AND THEY JUST LAUGH ABOUT IT?
ooo!!?

WE CAN'T OPEN THIS WITHOUT A KEY.
THESE BARS ARE TOO THICK FOR ME TO CUT THROUGH.
OH...

HEH HEH HEH HEH HEH!!
HAR HAR HAR HAR HAR HAR!!
HAR HAR HAR HAR HAR HAR!!

VERY FUNNY...
NOW HAND OVER THE KEYS TO THIS CAGE BEFORE I GET CRANKY.
HA HA
HA HA HA HA

THOSE GUYS ARE KINDA CREEPY.
HA HA HA HA

CHUNK!
!!

FWMP
NNGH...
!!?
BWA HA HA HA HA HA!!
HAR HAR HAR HAR HAR HAR!
WHAT THE--!? THAT HAND--!
ZOLO!?

SHCK
WHAT'S GOING ON...!?
FWIP!
THE HAND... IT'S FLOATING!
BA-BUMP
BA-BUMP
THE CHOP-CHOP FRUIT...!!!
!?
FWOM
FWOM

DOON!!

YOU CAN SLICE AND DICE ME, BUT YOU CAN'T KILL ME!!! I'M A CHOP-CHOP MAN!

THAT'S THE DEVIL FRUIT THAT I ATE!!!

HIS BODY IS BACK TO-GETHER AGAIN!
I THOUGHT THE STORIES ABOUT THE DEVIL FRUIT WERE JUST MYTHS!
...!!

CHOP-CHOP MAN!?
THAT GUY'S A FREAK!!
GUM-GUM MAN

SMRK
LOOKS LIKE I MISSED YOUR VITALS... BUT YOU STILL TOOK A SERIOUS WOUND!
RORONOA ZOLO! YOU NEVER HAD A CHANCE!

CAPTAIN BUGGY, YOU'RE THE GREATEST!
FINISH HIM! FINISH HIM!
EAAHH!
FWP FWP

I CAME TO SAVE LUFFY, NOW I'M THE ONE WHO NEEDS SAVING.
I HEARD THAT THIS CLOWN HAD EATEN DEVIL-TREE FRUIT... I SHOULD HAVE BEEN PREPARED...

NOT GOOD. THE TABLES HAVE TURNED...
IF I DON'T DO SOMETHING, THOSE TWO WILL END UP DEAD--AND SO WILL I!!

...

STABBING SOMEONE IN THE BACK... THAT'S FIGHTING DIRTY!!
YOU GOT THAT, BIG NOSE!??
GASP—!!! —!!!!
YOU FOOL! THAT'S THE ONE THING YOU NEVER–
YOU DARE TO CALL ME "BIG NOSE"!?

WOOSH!
!!
LUFFY!!!
GASP!
DA-DUM!!?
I SWEAR...
I'M GONNA CLOBBER YOU!!!
HEH HEH...
CLOBBER ME?

HA HA HA HA HA HA HA!! CLOBBER ME!!

DON'T MAKE ME LAUGH! YOU THREE ARE ABOUT TO DIE!!

HA HA HA HA HA!!

IT'S HOPELESS. WE'RE DEAD...

HA HA HA HA HA!!

NO WAY! I'M NOT GONNA DIE!!

AND JUST ***HOW*** DO YOU INTEND TO CLOBBER ME ***NOW***?
HA HA HA HA HA HA HA HA
AIN'T THAT A LAUGH, BOYS?

ZOLO!!
RUN!!!
HUH!?

WHAT? I'M NOT GOING ANYWHERE! WE'RE TRYING TO SAVE YOU!
THEY'LL KILL YOU THE MOMENT WE GO!
...

OH... GOTCHA...

READ THIS WAY
HE'S DESERTING US!? URGH! THAT'S WHY I HATE PIRATES! NOW I HAVE TO COME UP WITH AN ESCAPE PLAN!
AAARGGG
RORONOA ZOLO! YOU WON'T GET AWAY THAT EASILY!!
FWOOSH
CHOP-CHOP CANNON!
KLANG
KLANG
AH HA HA HA HA! ZOLO'S RUNNING AWAY!!
TP TP TP TP TP TP
HE WON'T ESCAPE CAP'N BUGGY!!!
UNGH!

HRRF!
PWURT
!!!
NO WAY...!!
AAAAH!
THE BIG CANNON'S POINTED AT US!!!
AAAAH!!
GYAAAH!
GYAA!
GYAA!
AND IT'S LOADED WITH ONE OF MY BUGGY BALLS!!
YAAAH!!!

YEAH!
LIGHT THIS THING!
HUNH?
WHOA!
R-RIGHT!!
HURRY!!
NO!!
LOOK OUT!!!

READ THIS WAY
NOW'S OUR CHANCE!
FSSH
WHO'RE YOU, ANYWAY?
FSSH
I'M...
...A THIEF.
FSSH
ACTUALLY...
SHE'S OUR NEW NAVIGATOR!
WHAT ARE YOU TALKING ABOUT!? ARE YOU CRAZY?
AND SHOULDN'T YOU BE TRYING TO GET OUT OF THAT CAGE?
OH, YEAH. MAYBE YOU'RE RIGHT...
...
NO PROBLEM...
YOU JUST STAY IN THE CAGE.

YOU'RE NOT GOING ANY-WHERE!
FSSH
FSSH
COFF
COFF
FWFF
FWFF
NNGH!!
ZOLO, DON'T DO THIS!
YOUR GUTS'LL SQUIRT OUT!
I DO THINGS MY OWN WAY!
SPURT!
THEN I'LL JUST SHOVE 'EM BACK IN!
HOW CAN YOU DO THIS?
SPURT!
!!

READ THIS WAY

SO DON'T GIVE ME ANY LIP ABOUT IT!

I DON'T GET IT! NO PIRATE WOULD SACRIFICE HIMSELF TO SAVE A FRIEND!

WHERE'D THEY GO!?
FWFF FF

THEY'RE GONE, CAP'N!
KRAKOOM
ZOLO, NAMI... EVEN THE CAGE!
IMPOSSIBLE! IT'S AN IRON CAGE! IT TOOK FIVE OF US TO MOVE IT!

OH NO!! IT'S GONE TOO!!
WHAT'S GONE!?

THE KEY TO THE CAGE...
SOME-ONE TOOK IT!

READ THIS WAY

KRASH!
OOF!

HUF HUF
PHEW...

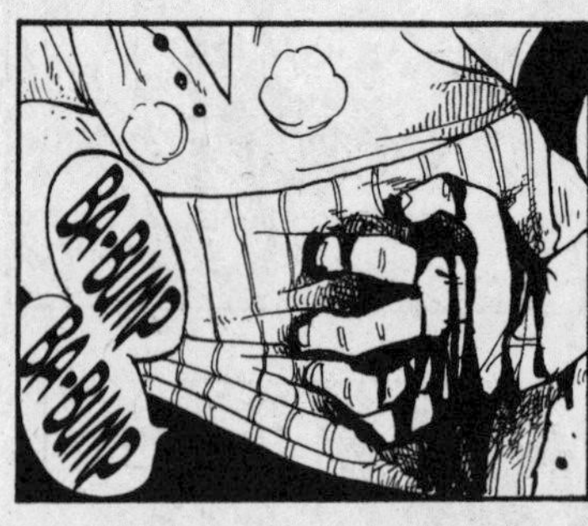
BA-BUMP
BA-BUMP

DARN IT!

KLANG

KLANG

THE TAVERN!?

EMPTY!

MAIN STREET!?

NOT HERE!

KLA

KLANG

IF ONLY I COULD GET OUT OF THIS CAGE!!!

WE'RE IN A... FINE MESS...

NOW WE GOTTA FINISH WHAT WE STARTED.

KRASH

NO MORE CLOWNING AROUND!!!

THOSE THREE ARE TRYING TO MAKE A FOOL OF ME!!!

WHO AM I!?
PIRATE CAPTAIN BUGGY THE CLOWN!!
DAMN STRAIGHT!

GRRRRRRR
CLEARLY WE'RE NOT DEALING WITH COMMON THIEVES!!!
I CONSIDER THIS A DECLARATION OF WAR!!!

One Piece Rough Sketch!

おおおっ!! モージさんだ!!
お呼びで？
バギー船長
モージさんの猛獣ショーだ!!!
グルルル…
バギー一味副船長 "猛獣使い"のモージ
のっし のっし
ロロノア・ゾロの首 私が取っても？
構わん

Chapter 12: DOG

LISTEN UP, CREW!
TA-DOOM
WE'VE STOLEN TONS OF BOOTY, AND OUR NAME BRINGS TERROR TO ALL WHO HEAR IT!

SO ARE WE GONNA LET THREE LITTLE LOSERS MAKE FOOLS OF US!?
NO SIR!!
I CAN'T HEAR YOU!!
NO SIR!!!
ALL RIGHT, PIPE DOWN!

IT'S TIME TO SHOW OUR ENEMIES JUST HOW TERRIFYING WE CAN BE!
BRING OUT THE "WILD ANIMAL SHOW"!

OOOOH! IT'S MOHJI!
CAPTAIN BUGGY...
...YOU CALLED?
IT'S TIME FOR MOHJI'S WILD ANIMAL SHOW!!
MOHJI! MOHJI!
MOHJI!
GRRRRR...!!
BUGGY'S FIRST MATE MOHJI THE LION TAMER
MOHJI! MOHJI! MOHJI!
MAY I TAKE RORONOA ZOLO'S HEAD?
TAKE ANY PART YOU WANT!

READ THIS WAY

WE SHOULD BE FAR ENOUGH FROM THAT TAVERN.

THEY PROBABLY WON'T CATCH UP TO US TOO SOON...
HUF
HUF
PLIP PLIP

WE GOT AWAY... FOR NOW...
BUT WHAT ARE WE GONNA DO ABOUT THIS CAGE?
KLANG
KLANG
KLANG
I CAN'T DO ANYTHING STUCK INSIDE THIS THING!
KRSS KRSS

IT'S NO USE... LOST TOO MUCH BLOOD...
FWUMP...!
...GOT TO... REST...

READ
THIS
WAY

PO——OM
HUH

WHAT'S WITH YOU, DOG?
......
DOG? HEY, A DOG!

IS IT REAL?
IT'S NOT MOVING...
WHO CARES...
IT'S HIS BUSINESS IF HE MOVES OR NOT.
OUR BUSINESS IS TO GET YOU OUT OF THERE.

MAYBE IT'S DEAD.
DOINK
!

CHOMP!!
YOW!!

DUMB DOG! LEMME GO, LEMME GO!!
LANG
GRRR ARR
CHOMP
CHOMP
KLANG
LUFFY, STOP PLAYING AROUND!
PURT

DUMB DOG!
......
LOST... TOO MUCH BLOOD!
FWOP...!
FLUMP...!

LOOK AT YOU TWO. NOT TO CRITICIZE, BUT...
...IS THE MIDDLE OF THE STREET REALLY THE BEST HIDING PLACE YOU COULD COME UP WITH?
SIGH

READ THIS WAY

HEY! IT'S OUR NAVIGATOR!
I NEVER AGREED TO THAT!

I JUST WANTED TO THANK YOU FOR SAVING ME...
THANK US?

HEY!
TINK

THE KEY!!!
YOU STOLE THE KEY TO THE CAGE!

HMPH.
YEAH, SURE...
I GOT THE STUPID KEY, BUT I LEFT THE MAP AND ALL THE TREASURE.

THIS IS GREAT! I THOUGHT I'D NEVER GET OUT OF HERE!

THEN THE RESCUE... WAS A SUCCESS... AFTER ALL!

ULP

CHONK
HEY...

...
...

...!
YIPE YIPE!
DUMB DOG!
KLANG
KLANG
GRRRR
KLOMP...!

SKRNCH
THAT'S NOT FOOD!! GIMME THAT KEY!!
COUGH IT UP!!

DON'T YOU PICK ON POOR OL' CHOU-CHOU!
THOOOM
DERN WHIPPER-SNAPPERS!
WHO'RE YOU, OLD TIMER?
CHOUCHOU?
WHO AM I?
I'M THE MAYOR OF THIS TOWN...
THAT'S WHO!
BAM
BOODLE
MAYOR OF PORT TOWN

WHERE'D YOU TAKE ZOLO?
HE'S RESTING. MY HOUSE IS JUST OVER THERE.
FRP
THAT BOY'S LOST A LOT OF BLOOD!

I TOLD 'IM THERE'S A DOCTOR AT THE REFUGEE SHELTER, BUT HE SAID HE JUST NEEDS A LITTLE SLEEP!!
SNORR
SNORR

THE DOG'S NAME IS CHOUCHOU?
THAT'S RIGHT.

WHY'S HE THE ONLY ONE LEFT IN TOWN?
HE'S GUARDING THE SHOP!
I JUST CAME TO FEED HIM.
OH! SO HE'S A GUARD DOG!
PET FOOD
CHOMP CHOMP
FOR A PET FOOD STORE...

READ THIS WAY

A GOOD FRIEND OF MINE OWNED THIS STORE.
ABOUT TEN YEARS AGO...
...HE AND CHOUCHOU OPENED THIS LITTLE SHOP.
PET FOOD
OPEN

THEY'VE GOT A LOT OF MEMORIES HERE
AND SO DO I...

CHOUCHOU! YOU'RE IN CHARGE WHILE I'M GONE.
DON'T EAT UP ALL THE MERCHAN-DISE, Y'HEAR!?
RUFF!

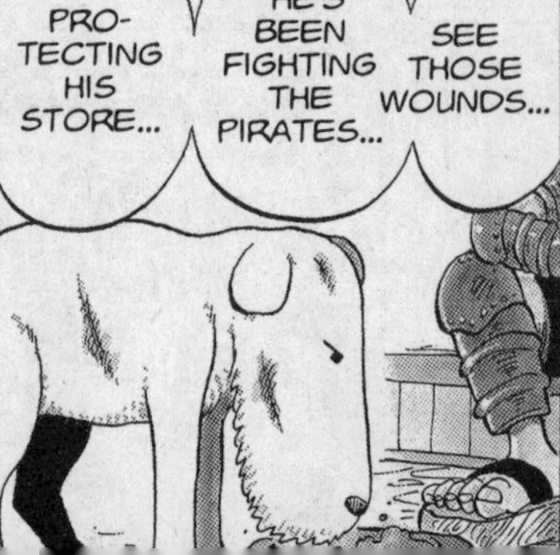
SEE THOSE WOUNDS...
HE'S BEEN FIGHTING THE PIRATES...
PRO-TECTING HIS STORE...

I'M SURE THIS SHOP MEANS A LOT TO HIS MASTER, BUT THIS IS JUST CRUEL.
IS HE AT THE REFUGEE SHELTER WITH THE OTHERS?

READ THIS WAY

NO, HE'S NOT...
HE GOT SICK AND PASSED ON.
!

HE WENT TO THE HOSPITAL THREE MONTHS AGO.
AWRIGHT, CHOUCHOU...
FOOD
YOU'RE IN CHARGE OF THE SHOP WHILE I'M IN THE HOSPITAL.
RUFF!

THE POOR THING...
YOU MEAN HE'S BEEN WAITING FOR HIS MASTER THIS WHOLE TIME?

THAT'S WHAT EVERYBODY SAYS, BUT THAT'S NOT WHAT I THINK.

READ
THIS
WAY

CHOU-CHOU'S A SMART DOG...
I THINK HE KNOWS HIS MASTER IS DEAD.
CHOMP CHOMP
...

THEN WHY DOES HE STILL GUARD THE STORE?
THIS IS HIS MASTER'S STORE...
IT'S HIS TREASURE.

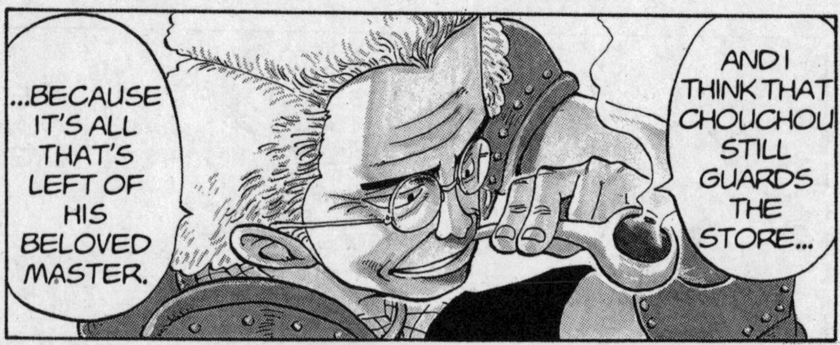
AND I THINK THAT CHOUCHOU STILL GUARDS THE STORE...
...BECAUSE IT'S ALL THAT'S LEFT OF HIS BELOVED MASTER.

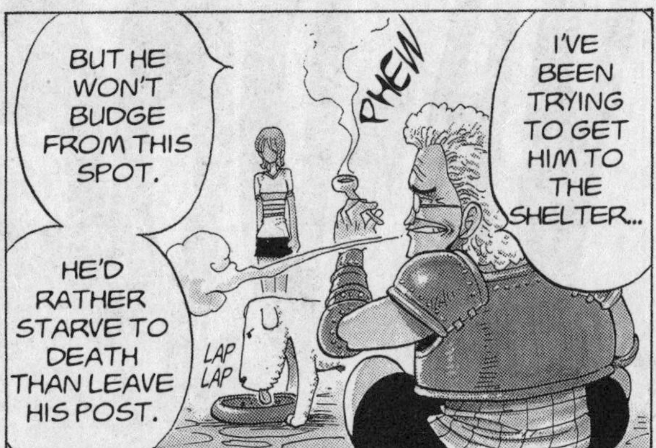
I'VE BEEN TRYING TO GET HIM TO THE SHELTER...
PHEW
BUT HE WON'T BUDGE FROM THIS SPOT.
HE'D RATHER STARVE TO DEATH THAN LEAVE HIS POST.
LAP LAP

...

ROOOWWRR...!!!
GASP!!
HUH?!

WHAT'S THAT HORRIBLE ROAR!?
I-IT MUST BE MOHJI, THE LION TAMER!!
ROWRR

SOME-THING'S COMING THIS WAY!
RUN!!!
TP TP TP TP TP TP
SIGH
GIVE ME THAT KEY, DOG!
WURF!

PA-DOOM...
WELL, WHAT HAVE WE HERE...?
I'M MOHJI, BUGGY'S FIRST MATE. THEY CALL ME THE LION TAMER!
GRRRRR...!!

HA HA HA... LOOKS LIKE YOUR FRIENDS ABAN-DONED YOU.
AND AFTER ALL THAT EFFORT TO GET YOU THIS FAR...

HEY, WHAT'S WITH THE WEIRD COSTUME?
WHAT!!?

CAPTAIN BUGGY IS PRETTY WORKED UP...
KRSS
KRSS
YOU GUYS STIRRED UP A REAL HORNETS' NEST.
GRRRRR...
GRRRR...

COSTUME!? THIS IS MY HAIR!!!

THAT JUST MAKES IT WEIRDER.
SHUT UP!

MAYBE YOU THINK YOU'RE SAFE IN THAT CAGE...
IF SO, THEN YOU REALLY DON'T KNOW WHO I AM...

I CAN EVEN CONTROL THAT MUTT.
THERE'S NOT AN ANIMAL ALIVE THAT I CAN'T CONTROL.
IS LUFFY PROVOKING THAT GUY?
IS THAT BOY ADDLE-BRAINED?

HA HA! DOG GOT YA!
YOU'RE JUST A NO-BODY THIEF...

YEOW!!
CHOMP!
SHAKE!

NO!
GRRRR...!!
NOW TELL ME WHERE RORONOA ZOLO IS.
YOU'RE NOTHING TO ME.

THEN DIE! GET HIM, RICHIE!
GRRROWR!!
CHONK
KRAK
!!
THE CAGE!
HOORAY! I'M FREE!
THAT BOY'S A GONER!
WOOSH
!?

FWAKOOOM
GROWWRR!
!!!
C'MON, RICHIE, LET'S GO FIND RORONOA ZOLO.
NOBODY COULD SURVIVE THAT. WELL, SERVES HIM RIGHT.
KILLING HIM WILL GIVE OUR REPU-TATION A BIG BOOST.
PLMP

WHAT'S WRONG...?
SNFF SNFF

SKRUF
I SEE... A PET FOOD STORE.
OKAY, FINE...
HAVE A SNACK, BUT BE QUICK ABOUT IT.
PET FOOD
!
GRRRR!

GRRR...!
GRRRR!

PHEW!
WOW! WHAT AN IMPACT!
HE KNOCKED ME THROUGH THAT HOUSE AND INTO THE STREET BEHIND IT!

BUT AT LEAST I'M OUT OF THAT CAGE!!

OKAY, NOW I'LL SHOW ALL OF THESE CLOWNS...

CHING

...AND MAKE THAT THIEF, NAMI, OUR NAVIGATOR!

VIKINGS, PART 2

✣ These guys were really scary. How scary were they? Well, they'd sweep out of an inlet, attack ships or villages, and slaughter everyone, even the local priests. They stole food and anything of value, and when they were done they set fire to everything they didn't want. They were unbelievable villians.

✣ But from their perspective, they were just trying to make a living. They brought the spoils of their piracy home to better their villages. This was "men's work." These people considered a lifetime of pillage and battle to be a good career.

✣ Some say the word Viking comes from "vik," meaning "creek" or "inlet"—meaning the people who attack from the inlets.

-VIKING-

Chapter 13:
TREASURE

HEY!

HUH?

HEY, KID! YOU'RE ALIVE!
HOW COULD YOU SURVIVE THAT!?
NO BIG DEAL.
?

BUT HOW? YOUR BODY DEMOLISHES A BUILDING AND YOU WALK AWAY WITHOUT A SCRATCH!? THAT'S CRAZY!
CRAZY IS GOOD.

WHY DID YOU ALL COME TO THIS TOWN ANYWAY? WHY TAKE ON PIRATES?

I JUST FIGURED OUT WHY I'M HERE.
I'M AFTER THE MAP OF THE GRAND LINE... AND A NAVIGATOR!!

RUFF!!
WHAT'S WITH THIS DOG?
RUFF!
RUFF!!
DOES HE THINK HE CAN STOP US FROM ENTERING THAT STORE?
PET FOOD
RUFF!
RUFF!

RUFF!! RUFF!!
RUFF!

DON'T TELL ME YOU'RE GUARDING THIS CRUMMY SHOP?
GRRRRR...

YOU LITTLE MUTT...

SKRSSK
YIPE!!
SWAP...

RUFF! RUFF!
RUFF!
SKRUF
SKRUF
GRRRRR!

LOOK, CHOUCHOU! THE STORE'S ALL FINISHED!
YOU AND ME WILL MAKE IT PROSPER TOGETHER!
RUFF!
PET FOOD
OPEN

CHOMP
!!
THWAK!!
FWUMP...!
BUSINESS IS AWFUL SLOW...
RUFF!
HAVING A ROUGH TIME, EH? FINE, THEN I'LL BUY SOME PET FOOD TO EAT!
HA HA HA! YOU LOOK LIKE A DOG, BUT I DIDN'T KNOW YOU ATE LIKE ONE, TOO!!
YOU IDIOT! I'M TRYING TO HELP YOU!

RUFF! RUFF!
MY-OH-MY!

YOU DON'T KNOW WHEN TO QUIT! IS YOUR FAVORITE FOOD IN THERE, DOGGY?

WE SOLD 100 BOXES TODAY!
RUFF!

CHOUCHOU! HOW MANY TIMES HAVE I TOLD YOU NOT TO EAT THE MERCHANDISE!

HEH HEH! THAT'S THE SMARTEST, BRAVEST DOG IN TOWN, MISS!
PET FOOD

AWRIGHT, CHOUCHOU. YOU'RE IN CHARGE OF THE SHOP WHILE I'M IN THE HOSPITAL.

GRRRR...
RUFF!
RUFF! RUFF!

I'M GOING TO LOOK FOR ZOLO.
I'D BETTER FIND HIM BEFORE THAT WEIRD COSTUME GUY DOES.
DON'T TALK CRAZY! NEXT TIME, THAT LION WILL EAT YOU ALIVE!

KRUNCH
KRUNCH
KRUNCH
RSK RSK

...STUB-BORN DOG BIT MY ARM...
I'M BLEED-ING!

WHAT KIND OF FOOL WOULD PIT A DOG AGAINST ME?
WELL, HE'LL NEVER SELL PET FOOD IN THIS TOWN AGAIN...

!
RUFF!
SHUF
SHUF

RUFF!
RUFF!

RUFF! RUFF! RUFF!
RUFF! RUFF! RUFF!
RUFF! RUFF!
...
RUFF!
RUFF! RUFF!
THIS IS HIS MASTER'S STORE...
KRASH
RUFF! RUFF!
IT'S HIS TREA-SURE.

RUFF!
RUFF! RUFF!
AND I THINK THAT CHOUCHOU STILL GUARDS THE STORE...

RUFF!
RUFF! RUFF!

RUFF! RUFF!
...BECAUSE IT'S ALL THAT'S LEFT OF HIS BELOVED MASTER.
RUFF!
RUFF! RUFF!

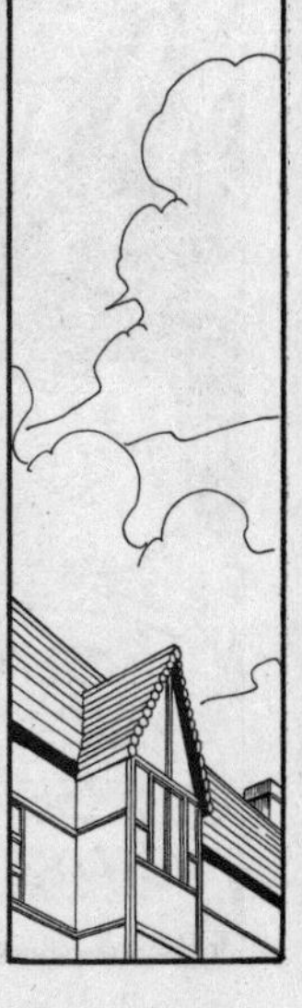

DOOM!!

...?
YOU!!
DIDN'T I JUST DEAL WITH YOU?

YOU SHOULD BE DEAD!!

IT TAKES MORE THAN A LITTLE KICK TO KILL ME!

I'M A RUBBER MAN!

RUBBER MAN? YOU'VE GOT THE DEVIL'S OWN LUCK, BOY. BUT THAT HIT MUST HAVE SCRAMBLED YOUR BRAINS...
YOU'D HAVE TO BE CRAZY...

TO TANGLE WITH ME AGAIN! RICHIE, BITE HIS HEAD OFF!!
KILL!
GRRRARARRR!!!
IT'LL TAKE MORE THAN THAT LION...
TO KILL ME!
SHWURK SHWURK!!
WHAT'RE YOU DOING TO YOUR ARMS!?
HOW CAN YOU--!?
GRMF!?
HRUNCH!!

FWOOP
FWOOP
FWOOP
FWOOP
GUM-GUM...
KRASH
...GAVEL!!!!

!!!?
RICHIE!!!

WHAT ARE YOU, YOU FREAK!?

A LONG TIME AGO, I ATE THE FRUIT OF THE GUM-GUM TREE!!

HMPH!

FWUMP

THE GUM-GUM TREE?

YOU ATE THE DEVIL'S FRUIT, LIKE CAPTAIN BUGGY!?

OKAY, OKAY! I'LL GIVE YOU ALL THE GOLD YOU WANT!!!
J-JUST LET ME APOLOGIZE AND GO! ALIVE!

IT'S TOO LATE FOR APOLOGIES...
THEY WON'T BRING THAT DOG'S TREASURE BACK!
WOOOSH

THAT'S WHY I CAME...
...TO CLOBBER YOU!
BOOM
WAAH! YOU'RE STRETCHING AGAIN!!!
GRAB
TAKE THIS!
AAAAHHHH! NOOOO! PLEASE!!!!
WAAAAAGH!
SREEEEEN

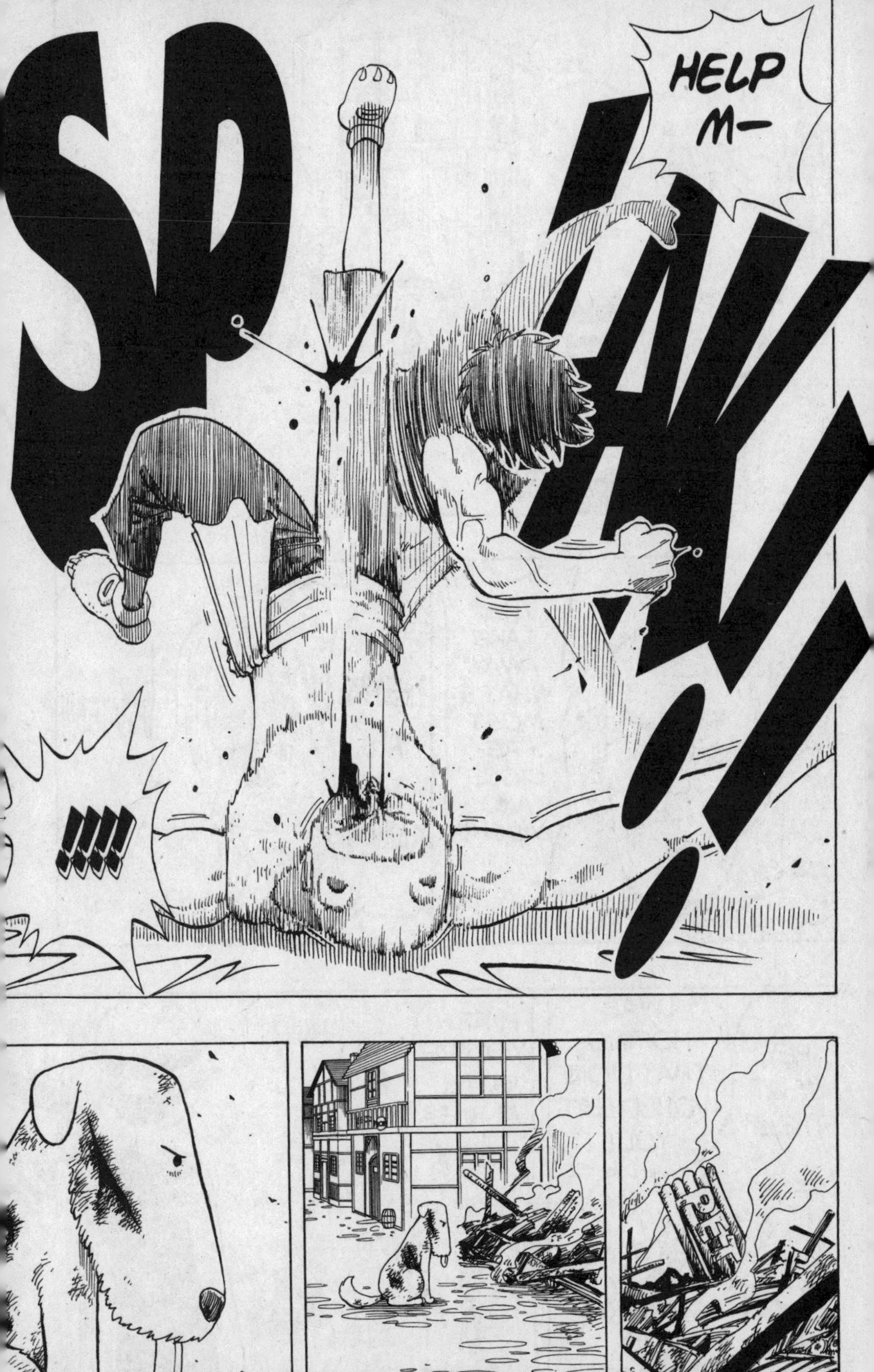
HELP M—
!!!!

PIRATES!!!
THEY'RE ALL THE SAME!!!
THEY TAKE AWAY WHAT'S MOST PRECIOUS AND LAUGH!!!
...

HUH?
!
SHUF
HMPH! YOU'RE STILL ALIVE?
I WAS HOPING THAT LION WOULD EAT YOU!
HEY, WHAT THE...?

READ THIS WAY

I OUGHTA KILL YOU RIGHT NOW, BEFORE YOU CAN GET A CREW AND GO PILLAGE SOME TOWN!
NOW, SIMMER DOWN!

YOU DON'T STAND A CHANCE AGAINST ME!
HUH!?
GRRR
PLFF

THEN LET'S HAVE IT OUT RIGHT NOW!!!
HEARTLESS PIRATE!
SHUF SHUF
CALM DOWN! WHAT'S WRONG WITH YOU!?

!
PLUNK!

HEY...

THAT'S ALL I COULD SAVE FOR YOU, BOY!
...
THE REST GOT EATEN, OR BURNED...

ULP!

HE FOUGHT THAT LION...
...FOR THE DOG'S SAKE!!
PETFOOD

YOU DID GOOD! YOU FOUGHT WELL!
I DIDN'T GET TO SEE YOU IN ACTION...
BUT I KNOW YOU DID GOOD!

...
CHOMP
PETFOOD

SHUF SHUF

FWP

RUFF!
!
THANKS...
GOOD LUCK TO YOU, TOO!

RUFF!!!
RUFF!!!

HMPH...

MOHJI WAS DEFEATED!?
'AT'S RIGHT, CAP'N!
Drinker Pub
READY MY SPECIAL BUGGY BALLS!!!
TEATIME'S OVER, KIDDIES! WE'RE GOING TO LIGHT UP THIS TOWN!! UNTIL THERE'S NOTHING LEFT!!!

One Piece Rough Sketch!

どチキショーが
畜がさんぞォ!!!
もくもく
ゴホ
ゴホ
ばふ
ばふっ
オオ…!!
おいゾロ
いいよ!
腹わた
飛び出るぞ
おれはおれの
やりてェ様に
やる!
飛び出たら
しまえばいい
何で
ここまで…!!!
ゴオ…

Chapter 14:
RECKLESS

READ THIS WAY

AHOY! FIRST MATE MOHJI'S BACK!

S-SORRY... CAPTAIN...
I'VE GOT TO TELL HIM THAT THE KID IS A RUBBER MAN...
WEEZE WEEZE
HUF HUF
...THE KID... CAP'N... BUGGY...

THE KID!? THE KID IN THE STRAW HAT BEAT YOU!?
NOT ZOLO!?
WUP WUP
THE KID...
...UNDER... ESTIMATED HIM.
G-GOT TO TELL HIM...
WEEZE WEEZE
HUF HUF
CAP'N... SIR...
BEWARE... THE RUB-

...RUB-
WORB WORB
...RUB...!!

FWUMP
...MAN...

READ THIS WAY

WHAT'D HE SAY?
MOHJI WAS TRYING TO TELL US SOMETHING.
HE COULD BARELY STAND! MUST HAVE BEEN IMPORTANT...
"BEWARE THE RUB!?"
WHAT KIND OF RUB COULD DO THAT TO A MAN!?

HMM... THAT BOY MUST HAVE USED SOME DIABOLICAL RUBBING TECHNIQUE ON HIM...!
!
AR! THE SKIPPER'S GOT IT!

DARN YOU, MOHJI!
BEATEN BY A MASSEUR?! IF THIS GETS OUT, OUR REPUTATION'S SCUTTLED!
LOAD THE BUGGY BALLS, YOU SWABS!! WE'VE A TOWN TO DESTROY!!
AYE AYE, CAP'N BUGGY!
RUBBER MAN...

TMP
TMP

THE REFUGE OF THE TOWNS-PEOPLE
TMP
TMP
TMP
WHAT'S THAT!?
HEY! IT'S CHOUCHOU FROM THE PET FOOD SHOP!

WE'RE GLAD YOU'RE OKAY, BOY! WE WERE WORRIED ABOUT YOU.
IT'S CHOUCHOU!
HE'S HURT BAD. CURSED PIRATES!
LET'S TAKE CARE OF HIS WOUNDS.

BUT WHERE'S THE MAYOR?
MURMUR
MURMUR
THAT'S RIGHT...! MAYOR BOODLE WENT TO FEED CHOUCHOU.
WHAT'S CHOUCHOU DOING HERE WITHOUT HIM?

YOU DON'T THINK SOMETHING HAPPENED TO THE MAYOR?
THIS ISN'T GOOD...
I'LL GO FIND HIM!
MURMUR MURMUR
NOW DON'T GO OFF HALF-COCKED! THE MAYOR'S TOO CLEVER TO LET HIMSELF GET CAPTURED.
HE KNOWS THIS TOWN BETTER THAN ANYONE.

BUT HE ALSO **CARES** ABOUT THE TOWN MORE THAN ANYONE. MAYBE TOO MUCH.
DON'T TAKE ANY UNNECESSARY RISKS NOW, MAYOR.
WHAT MATTERS IS THAT WE'RE ALL SAFE. AS LONG AS WE ALL SURVIVE, WE CAN REBUILD THIS TOWN.
I KNOW, I KNOW. I'M JUST GOING TO FEED CHOUCHOU!
I WARNED HIM NOT TO TAKE ANY RISKS. I JUST HOPE HE HEARD ME.

?
STP

READ
THIS
WAY

SORRY
I YELLED
AT YOU!

HUH?

THAT'S OKAY.
I KNOW YOU
LOST
SOMEONE TO
PIRATES.
I
UNDER-
STAND...
NOT
THAT I
WANT TO
HEAR THE
DETAILS
OR ANY-
THING...

...

UNGRRRR!!

I
CAN'T
STANDS
IT NO
MORE!!!
AAAAH!
HUH!?

I CAN'T STAND ANY MORE OF THEIR CRUEL BULLYING! NOT AFTER THE WAY CHOUCHOU AND THIS KID FOUGHT BACK SO BRAVELY!
WHAT KIND OF MAYOR STANDS BACK AND WATCHES HIS TOWN BE DESTROYED!?
MAYOR, PLEASE! CALM DOWN!
BWAAH!
SOMETIMES, A MAN'S GOTTA DO WHAT A MAN'S GOTTA DO!
ISN'T THAT RIGHT, SONNY?
DOOM
THAT'S RIGHT!!
YOU SAID IT, OLD MAN!!

FORTY YEARS OF HARD WORK!!
?
DON'T ENCOURAGE HIM!!
THIS PLACE WAS A WILDERNESS WHEN WE GOT HERE.
SHAAA

"WE'LL BUILD OUR TOWN RIGHT HERE!"
"WE'LL FORGET OUR OLD TOWN THAT THE PIRATES DESTROYED."
!

AT FIRST, IT WAS JUST A FEW HOMES.

BUT SLOWLY OUR NUMBERS GREW.

WE WORKED HARD, CLEARED THE LAND. OVER TIME PEOPLE CAME AND OPENED UP SHOPS.

HENKUTSU

TA-DA

AND LOOK AT US NOW! WE'RE A THRIVING PORT!

WE OLD TIMERS BUILT THIS TOWN FROM NOTHING!

IT'S ***OUR*** LIFE'S WORK!

...

THIS TOWN AND ITS PEOPLE ARE MY TREASURE!

I'D BE A SORRY EXCUSE FOR A MAYOR IF I DIDN'T TRY TO PROTECT THE TOWN!
I'M GONNA FIGHT!!!

FIRE THE BUGGY BALL!!!!
!!!?

KAB

OOOOOM
ARRGH!
KYAA!!
...!!
NNGH!
MY HOUSE! IT'S RUINED!
HEY!
ZOLO WAS SLEEPING IN THERE!

WHOOO...!!
....!!!
!
KLAK KLAK
HUH?
COULD THE KID WITH THE BELLY-BAND HAVE SURVIVED THAT!?
HEY, ZOLO!!! ARE YOU ALIVE!?
UNGHH!
TA-DA!
THAT'S ONE HECK OF AN ALARM CLOCK!

READ
THIS
WAY

HEY!
YOU'RE ALIVE!

...
HOW COULD ANYONE LIVE THROUGH THAT!?

...!!
THAT TEARS IT!
FWAP!!
MAYOR!
WOOO...
I CAN'T TAKE ANY MORE! I WON'T LOSE A SECOND TOWN TO THOSE SEA RATS!

THESE PIRATES SHOW UP, THINK THEY CAN DO AS THEY PLEASE...
GRR
BUT I WON'T LET 'EM WRECK FORTY YEARS OF HARD WORK!!!
I'M THE MAYOR!!!
I WON'T TAKE THIS SITTING DOWN!

IT'S TIME TO FIGHT!
MAYOR! WAIT, PLEASE!!
LET ME GO, GIRLIE!
GETTING YOURSELF KILLED WON'T ACCOMPLISH ANYTHING! YOU'RE BEING RECKLESS!!
BAM!
I KNOW I'M BEING RECKLESS!!!!
!

ARGHH!!
BUGGY THE CLOWN!!
PREPARE TO FACE THE MAYOR!
TMP TMP TMP TMP

THE MAYOR...
...HE WAS CRYING!!
IT DIDN'T LOOK THAT WAY TO ME!

THINGS ARE FINALLY GONNA GET FUN!
HA HA HA! YEAH!
THIS IS NO LAUGHING MATTER!
DON'T WORRY, I LIKE THAT OLD MAN!
I WON'T LET HIM GET KILLED!

HOW CAN YOU JUST STAND THERE LAUGHING? WHAT DO YOU GET OUT OF THIS ANYWAY?

WE'RE HEADED FOR THE "GRAND LINE"!

WE'LL STEAL THAT MAP BACK, AND THEN WE CAN GO THERE TOGETHER!

JOIN UP WITH US!
YOU WANT THE MAP AND ALL THAT TREASURE, RIGHT?
!
...
I WON'T BECOME A PIRATE!

SW AP!

LET'S JUST SAY WE'LL "JOIN FORCES"...

WORK TOGETHER FOR A COMMON GOAL!!

NOW FOR THE SECOND SALVO!
AYE AYE, CAP'N!
AIM! FI--
Drinker Pub
BUGGY THE CLOWN!!!
GET OUT HERE! NOW!!!
WHO DARES?

YOU'RE COMING TOO?
WHAT ABOUT YOUR WOUNDS?
THEY GOT BETTER.
THAT'S IMPOSSIBLE!
FWP

I'M MORE WORRIED ABOUT MY REPUTATION THAN MY GUTS, RIGHT NOW. I'VE GOT A SCORE TO SETTLE!
LET'S DO IT.

I CAN'T WAIT!
KRAK
KRAK
YOU TWO ARE CRAZY!

VIKINGS, PART 3

✤ When I was a kid, I used to enjoy watching an animated tv seres called **Chiisa na Viking Bikke** ("Little Viking Vicke"). The show was about the adventures of a Viking boy named Vicke, who wasn't very strong but was very clever, and a group of Vikings who were very strong but not so smart. Their adventures were very fun and entertaining.

Mother Ylva
Vicke
Ga ha ha ha ha!
Vicke's father (the Captain)
Geh Heh heh!
Sven, the mean guy (enemy of Vicke and the others)
Musician
He's always saying this.
That's impressive!
Merry Men

✤ It aired over 15 years ago, so a lot of people of my generation (I'm 23) remember it from childhood. If it ever gets rebroadcast, you should definitely check it out! That's probably how I started liking pirates.

Chapter 15:

GONG

READ THIS WAY

Drinker Pub

DA-DOOM!!

WHO ARE YOU... AND WHAT'S YOUR DEATH WISH?

I'M BOODLE, AND I'VE BEEN MAYOR OF THIS TOWN SINCE YOU WERE PILLAGING NURSERIES!

I'M HERE TO CHALLENGE YOU!

...
HMM

BWA HA HA HA HA HA HA!
HA HA HA HA HA HA HA
!
DOES HE REALLY THINK HE CAN BEAT THE CAPTAIN!?

CAP'N BUGGY...
GLUP
WHAT IS IT, CABAJI?
LEAVE HIM TO ME, SIR.

SIK SIK SIK
WHY, KEELHAUL ME! IT'S CABAJI THE ACROBAT!
YAAY!

LOOK AT 'IM GO!
AWUP AWUP AWUP
SPROING!

IT'S BEEN A WHILE.
WSSH WSSH
I DON'T WANT TO GET RUSTY...!
AYE! GO GET'IM, CABAJI!!!
CABAJI!!! CABAJI!!!
BUGGY'S SECOND MATE CABAJI THE ACROBAT
...
KREEK
AVAST, FOOL! HE CHALLENGED ME!
YOU STAY OUT OF THIS.

ARG! WE WON'T BE SEEING CABAJI'S ACROBATIC SHOW!
...
BOO BOO
WHY ARE YOU CHALLENGING ME!?
A LITTLE OLD TO BE MAKING A NAME FOR YOURSELF, AREN'T YOU?
THIS TOWN IS MY TREASURE, AND I'M GOING TO PROTECT IT!!!
HUH?
YOU SENILE OLD FOOL! THE ONLY TREASURE HERE IS FOR TERMITES! GOLD AND JEWELS ARE TREASURE!
GYAHAHAHAHAHA
TREASURE SPARKLES AND MAKES ITS POSSESSOR A KING!
THIS DUMP OF YOURS DOESN'T SPARKLE, IT ROTS!
ENOUGH OF YOUR NONSENSE!!!

SHUT UP, YOU SEA SQUIRT!
I DON'T EXPECT YOU TO UNDERSTAND MY FEELINGS FOR THIS TOWN!!!
NOW GET DOWN HERE!
ARRG
GET DOWN THERE?
WOOSA
WHY SHOULD I!?
!!?
THR
UNK

READ THIS WAY
YAHOO!
HYAAA HA HA HA HA!!
GACK GACK!
AYE, CAP'N!!
FWUP
FWUP
...!!!
Drinker Pub
Y-YOU... M-MONSTER!!!
TH-THIS IS...
...N-NOTHING!
WAP
WAP WAP
WAP
ARRGGH!
WHAT'S THAT?! YOU TRYING TO BEAT ME...
...BY PUNCHING YOURSELF IN THE THROAT!?
SQUEEZE!!
NNGH!
...

YOU DARE TO ORDER ME DOWN THERE!? DO YOU KNOW WHO YOU'RE TALKING TO?
ANSWER ME! WHAT'S MY NAME!?

I CAN'T DIE! NOT BEFORE I GET REVENGE!

NN...NNGH!

SOON, I SHALL RULE THE GRAND LINE!!

AND ALL THE GLITTERING TREASURE WILL BE MINE!!

ALL THE TREASURE IN THE WORLD! I'LL HAVE IT ALL, NOBODY ELSE!!

YAAHHRRRR!!!

THIS MISERABLE, STINKING TOWN IS YOUR TREASURE, EH?
THEN BE GLAD YOU WON'T LIVE TO SEE WHAT I DO TO IT!
!!
W-WHY YOU! CURSE YOU!
COME DOWN AND FIGHT LIKE A MAN!
YOU'RE NOT WORTH THE EFFORT!
C'MON!!
WOOO
!!
Drinker Pub
I WON'T LET YOU WRECK THIS TOWN!!
COME DOWN AND FIGHT ME!
!
HUH?
TWITCH!

!
THE KID IN THE STRAW HAT!
DOOM!
HACK! KOFF! KOFF!
I'M BACK!
I TOLD YOU I'D CLOBBER YOU!

FWUNK
I DON'T BELIEVE IT!
YOU TWO MUST ENJOY PAIN...
BUT THIS TIME YOU WON'T ESCAPE ME!!!
HAVE FUN FIGHTING, BOYS...
I'M JUST HERE FOR THE MAP AND THE TREASURE!
WHATEVER...

YOU YOUNG WHIPPER-SNAPPERS...
YOU'RE OUTSIDERS... **KOFF**... NOT YOUR FIGHT!
!
THIS IS **MY** BATTLE!

IT'S **MY** TOWN AND **I'LL** PROTECT IT!
FWISH
SO DON'T INTER-FERE!!!

!!
?!!
THWAK

MAYOR!?
HUH!?
...
...!!
SLUMP!!
FWUMP!!
ARGH!
YOU--!!
PAT
PAT
WHOSE SIDE ARE YOU ON!?
WHY'D YOU DO THAT TO THE MAYOR!?

GRIN

HE WAS IN THE WAY!!!

...!!

GOOD THINKING...
HE WOULD HAVE GOTTEN HIMSELF KILLED...
HE'LL BE SAFER UNCON-SCIOUS.
YOU'RE TOO RECKLESS!

STOMP
HEY YOU!!!
GASP!
BIG NOSE!!!
!!??
KILL HIM!!! GIVE 'IM THE BUGGY BALL!!!
GASP!!!
...!!!

FIRE!!!
YOU IDIOT! DON'T YOU KNOW WHEN TO SHUT UP!?
LUFFY! GET OUT OF THE WAY!! YOU'RE GONNA GET HIT!!!
THAT MEASLY CANNON-BALL'S...
...NOT GONNA WORK ON ME!
SMIRK

HUFF
GUM-GUM...
!!?
...BALLOON!!!

GGNNNN
...!!

...!?

WHAT THE HECK *IS* THAT GUY?!

HE TOOK A DIRECT HIT FROM A BUGGY BALL!

BOI

VWOOOO

NNG!!

AND HE BOUNCED IT BACK!!!!!

YOU COULD HAVE AT LEAST TOLD US WHAT YOU WERE PLANNING...

rker Pub

AAARRRGGGH!!!!!
KA-BOOM!!
MADE ME WORRY FOR NOTHING...
...WHAT ARE YOU!?
THAT EVENS THE ODDS A LITTLE!
LET'S GET 'EM!

One Piece Rough Sketch!

こんなとこで笑っててどっからその自信がわくのよ!!
おれ達が目指すのは"偉大なる航路"
これからその海図をもう一度奪いに行く!!
仲間になってくれ!
海図いるんだろ? 宝も
!
…
私は海賊にはならないわ!!
"手を組む"って言ってくれる?
お互いの目的の為に!!

Chapter 16:

VERSUS BUGGY'S CREW!

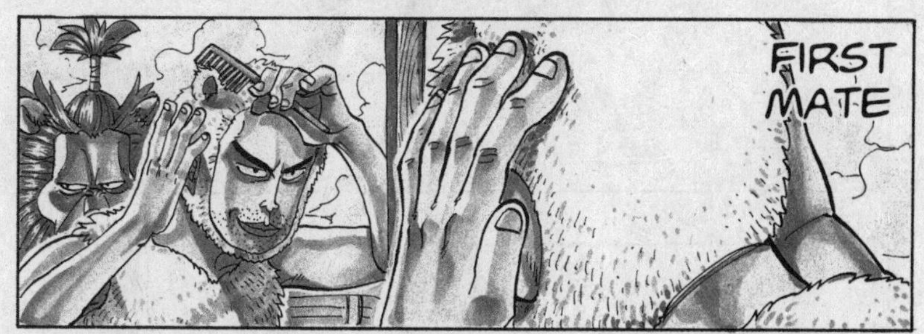
FIRST
MATE

CAPTAIN

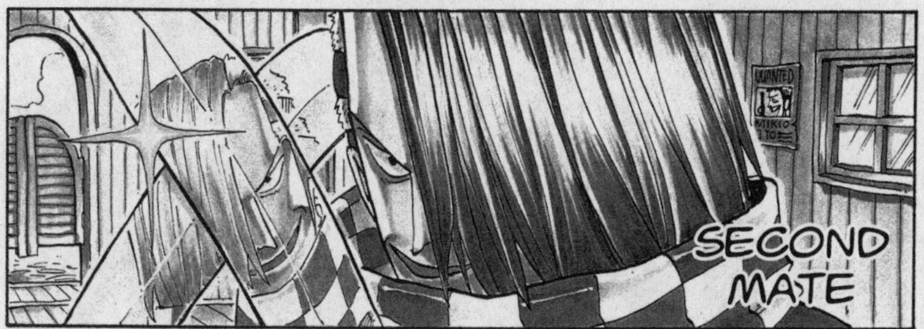
WANTED
SECOND
MATE

KRAAAASH...!

THUD...
KLANK...
KRAK...

WOW. I ***THOUGHT*** THERE WAS SOMETHING STRANGE ABOUT YOU...
...I MEAN, YOU DID PILE-DRIVE A LION!

WHAT KIND OF HUMAN BEING COULD DO THAT?!
HOW CAN YOU INFLATE YOURSELF LIKE A BALLOON!?

DA-DOOM
!
KLAK KLAK KLAK!!
...!!

THAT WAS THE GUM-GUM...
...BALLOON!!
DA—DA
BUT HOW DO YOU DO IT!?
IDIOT!!

UH-OH...
GASP!

YOU'VE GOT SOME NERVE...

HE'S USING HIS MEN AS SHIELDS...

CAP'N, THIS IS THE WORST DISGRACE WE'VE SUFFERED SINCE YOU FORMED OUR CREW...
I'M SO MAD, I CAN'T EVEN SPEAK...

KLAK KLAK
!
UNH... WHERE AM I...
WHAT THE HELL HAPPENED!?
MOHJI... YOU'RE STILL ALIVE?

!?
CABAJI! WHAT'RE YOU DOING TO RICHIE!?

THE KITTY?
FWUMP
I WAS USING HIM AS A SHIELD. DIDN'T WANT TO SOIL MY RAIMENT.

RICHIE!? ARE YOU OKAY!?
KOFF
KOFF

VREEEN

GRROWRRR!
GULP!!
TREMBLE TREMBLE
WHY YOU...!!
SHIVER SHIVER

GASP! IT'S THE KID IN THE STRAW HAT!! CAP'N BUGGY, WATCH OUT FOR HIM!!
HE'S GOT SPECIAL POWERS FROM EATING THE DEVIL FRUIT-- JUST LIKE YOU!!! HE'S A RUBBER MAN!!!

RUBBER MAN!?
YEP... SEE?
WOING

THE DEVIL FRUIT!!!

THAT'S WHY MY BUGGY BALL BOUNCED OFF OF HIM!
GRAB
HAH...
MOHJI, IF YOU **KNEW** THAT...

WHY DIDN'T YOU TELL ME!?
I TRIED TO!

GYAAAA!

WHOOSH

!

OUTTA MY WAY!!!

OUTTA MY WAY, FUZZY!

SHUU...

!!!

SKROOSH
THE BATTLE BEGINS!!
WHOA!
...!!
WHOOO
BUGGY'S SECOND MATE, CABAJI THE ACROBAT!!
I'LL CUT 'EM TO MINCE-MEAT, CAP'N!!
!
RERKRERKRERK
KRANG!!
!?

IF IT'S A SWORD DUEL YOU WANT, I'M YOUR MAN!
RORONOA ZOLO, AS ONE SWORDSMAN TO ANOTHER...
IT WILL BE AN HONOR TO CUT YOU DOWN.

!
THROB

HEY, ZOLO! MAYBE YOU SHOULD REST.
LET ME HANDLE HIM.

HE COULDN'T HAVE HEALED YET FROM THE WOUNDS THE CAPTAIN GAVE HIM. I'M SURPRISED HE CAN EVEN STAND...
HEH HEH...
"THE BREATH OF DEATH"!
WAGH!

READ THIS WAY

...!!

WOOSH!!

GASP!

OOH...!!

FWAK!!!!!!

READ THIS WAY

ARRRGGHH!!!

YEEOWW!!
HMM... I DIDN'T THINK I KICKED YOU THAT HARD...
HEHHEHHEH!

THAT'S DIRTY! YOU'RE AIMING FOR HIS INJURIES!!

I CALL MY NEXT CIRCUS TRICK...
HRASP HRASP

"MURDER AT THE STEAM BATH"!!

READ THIS WAY

WHAT KIND OF CIRCUS TRICK IS THAT!?
HUF HUF
BA-BA-BUMP
SSHH SSHH
YOU'RE JUST KICKING UP DUST!!
CHANK!
SPLURT

HEH HEH...
HUH?

KERWAP!!
!!!
UNGAAAH!!
SPUR
HE DID IT AGAIN!!
WHAT KIND OF MAN SCREAMS LIKE A WOMAN?
....!!
SLUMP

SO YOU'RE THE BIG SCARY "PIRATE HUNTER." WELL, THIS'LL TEACH YOU TO MESS WITH CAP'N BUGGY'S CREW.

RERK RERK

YOUR MATEY'S ODD TALENTS CAUSED US QUITE A BIT OF TROUBLE.

HOW CAN YOU JUST STAND THERE AND WATCH YOUR FRIEND GET KILLED!?

ZOLO'S HURT BAD! HOW'S HE SUPPOSED TO FIGHT!?

...

HUFF!!

HUFF...!! HUFF...!!

PREPARE TO BE **WELL DONE!!**

FWOOSH

RORONOA ZOLO!!

UNGH!?

HOW...?

YEAH!!

!

!??

YOU'RE A VERY ANNOYING PERSON...

SWIP

HUF

I HOPE YOU ENJOYED KICKING MY WOUND...

SLISH!!
!
!?
WHAT!!!
HE CUT HIMSELF!?
OUCH!
!

HOOPH!!!

MY GOAL IS TO BE THE WORLD'S GREATEST SWORDSMAN...
WHAT'RE YOU TALKING ABOUT...?
DRIP
SPLIP

IS THAT ENOUGH OF A HANDICAP FOR YOU?

CHUNK

NOW I'LL SHOW YOU SOME REAL SWORDPLAY.

WOW! ZOLO'S COOL!!

HMPH...
SO, RORONOA ZOLO...
YOU WANT TO MAKE A FOOL OUT OF *ME*?

One Piece Rough Sketch!

スタッ
最近どうも
ギュルルル…
腕がナマッてましてね…!!
カバジッ!! カバジッ
うおおお やっちまえ カバジさん!!
バギー一味No2
参謀長
"曲芸のカバジ"
ガッ!!
…
バカ野郎 ご指命は おれだぜ
さがってろ!!

Chapter 17:

HIGH LEVEL, LOW LEVEL

DA
PLIP
DRIP
TO ANYONE WHO CALLS HIMSELF A SWORDSMAN!!
I CAN'T LOSE, NOT EVEN ONCE...
GET 'IM, ZOLO!!
YEAH!
I'M FEELING FAINT JUST WATCHING THIS!

READ THIS WAY

SO YOU INJURED YOURSELF AS INSURANCE FOR YOUR REPUTATION... WELL, DON'T WORRY...
YOUR WOUNDS ARE SEVERE. THEY'LL MAKE AN EXCELLENT EXCUSE WHEN YOU LOSE.

GA-SHEEN!!

IT'S THE OTHER WAY AROUND!!

IF I LOSE TO THE LIKES OF YOU WHEN MY WOUNDS ARE ONLY THIS LIGHT...

THEN I MAY AS WELL GIVE UP MY DREAM RIGHT NOW.

SMIRK

....!!
YOU SCURVY DOG!!
...

READ
THIS
WAY

HEY!
PWAP!
HUH?

THAT SHACK BEHIND THE RUINS OF THE TAVERN...
THAT'S WHERE THEY KEEP THEIR TREASURE.

AND BUGGY'S PROBABLY GOT THE MAP OF THE GRAND LINE.
SHAAOOO

I'LL GET THEIR TREASURE AND MAKE MY ESCAPE.
I'VE GOT TO DO IT NOW, WHILE THEY'RE ALL KNOCKED OUT...

WHETHER YOU GUYS WIN OR LOSE THIS BATTLE...
I DON'T REALLY CARE!

READ THIS WAY

BUT IF YOU DO GET THAT MAP FROM BUGGY...
THEN— AND ONLY THEN— WILL I CONSIDER TEAMING UP WITH YOU AGAIN...

GOOD LUCK, BOYS! SEE YA!
TMP TMP
WOW! THANKS!

RORONOA ZOLO!! HAVE A TASTE OF THE GREATEST OF ALL MY CIRCUS TRICKS!!

...

WHRR

...

AND NOW "THE DANCE OF A HUNDRED KAMIKAZE TOPS"!!!
!
CIRCUS TRICK: "A HIKE IN THE MOUNTAINS."
RERK RERK
RERK RERK
ZOOM!

READ THIS WAY
...!
WAK
WAK
WAK WAK
!
FWOOSH
CIRCUS TRICK: "FIRE-WORKS IN THE COOL SUMMER BREEZE."
BOUND!

"STING OF THE UNICYCLE"!!
ZWEEEN
WOW! HE'S WAY UP THERE!
!
...
SWAP

LOW-FLYING CHOP-CHOP CANNON!!
KA-BOOM!!
!!
WHOOSH
CABAJI!!
I'LL HOLD ZOLO DOWN!! YOU FINISH HIM OFF!!
WITH PLEASURE!
WHOOOOSH!
DAMN...!!

STOMP
?!!
LUFFY!
ARRGHH!

DOOM

KEEP YOUR MITTS OUT OF ZOLO'S DUEL!

YOU LITTLE...
GRIN
HEH...

I DON'T NEED THE CAPTAIN TO LEND ME A HAND TO KILL YOU!!

!!
HMPH!
HUFF HUFF...
BA-BUMP BA-BUMP
I'VE HAD ENOUGH...
HUF
HUF
?!
I'M TIRED...

READ THIS WAY

YOU'RE TIRED? HEH HEH HEH... WHAT'S WRONG? ANEMIC?
SO YOU'VE FINALLY GIVEN UP! WELL, I'M NOT SURPRISED...
IT'S AMAZING YOU CAN STILL STAND IN YOUR CONDITION.

KA
?!!!
UNGH...!!!
THWACK

YOU'VE GOT IT WRONG. WHAT I'M TIRED OF...
ARE YOUR STUPID CIRCUS TRICKS!!!
...!
VERY WELL! NO MORE TRICKS! I'LL FINISH YOU NOW...
WITH MY **REAL** SWORDS-MANSHIP!!!
WSH!!
ONI...
SWURP

GIRI!!!*

* ONIGIRI = "DEMON SLASH!"

CABAJI!!!

GGH...! HOW COULD THESE COMMON THIEVES HAVE BEATEN US? WE'RE THE BUGGY PIRATE GANG—THE SCOURGE OF THE SEAS!!

HOW COULD THINGS HAVE GONE THIS FAR...?

FWUMP!!

WE'RE NOT *COMMON* THIEVES...
WOMP
HUF
HUF

WE'RE PIRATES!

KLANK

KLANK

LUFFY...
I'M GOING TO SLEEP NOW.

GO AHEAD AND SLEEP!
I'LL TAKE IT FROM HERE!
TOING

READ THIS WAY

YOU GUYS...
...CALL YOUR-SELVES *PIRATES!?*

THAT'S RIGHT!
NOW HAND OVER THE MAP OF THE GRAND LINE!!

SO THAT'S WHAT YOU'RE AFTER. WELL, A COUPLE OF LILY-LIVERED, NO-NAME PIRATES LIKE YOU WON'T LAST A DAY ON THE GRAND LINE!!
WHAT DO YOU PLAN TO DO THERE!? GO SIGHT-SEEING!?

I'M GONNA BE KING OF THE PIRATES.

HURF ACK HAR
...!!!
BOOM

DON'T BE A FOOL!

IF YOU'RE KING OF PIRATES, THEN WHAT AM I!? GOD OF THE PIRATES!?

THE WORLD'S TREASURE WILL BE MINE! SO FORGET IT!

OKAY, HURRY UP AND ATTACK ME.
I'M GETTING BORED.
KRAK KRAK
TA-

YOU'LL SOON REGRET YOUR WORDS, RUBBER BOY!
FWOOSH
CHEENG!
...!!

YOU AND YOUR STRAW HAT REMIND ME OF HIM WHEN HE WAS YOUNGER...
THAT INSOLENT DOG WITH THE RED HAIR!!!

...RED HAIR!?

Let's make a Sproingy Luffy!

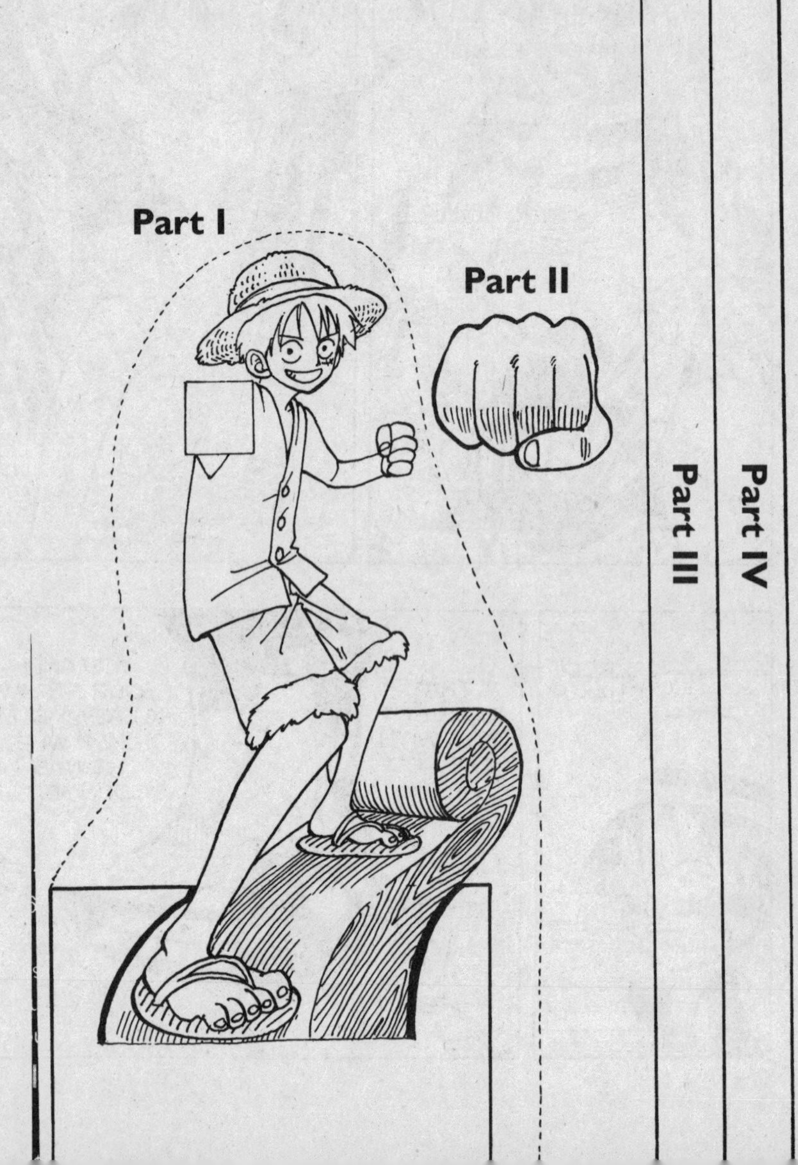

Part I
Part II
Part III
Part IV

How to make a Sproingy Luffy:

You need:
Scissors - Glue or paste - Crayons, markers, or colored pencils - Stiff paper - The strong will to make Sproingy Luffy

Instructions:

1. Color! To start out, color the various parts of Luffy. (Have fun!) Use flesh color for Parts II, III and IV. People who don't like messing up their books can make a photocopy to color and cut out instead.

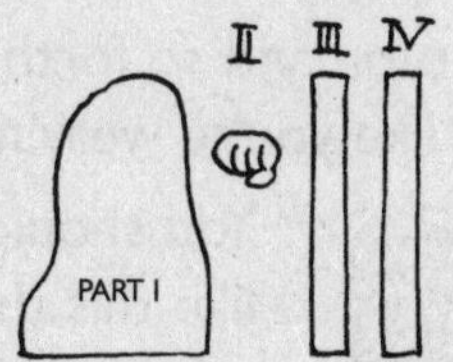
II
III
IV
PART I

2. Cut it out! Cut out Part I along the dotted line, and cut out the pieces for Parts II, III and IV, following the lines.
3. Paste Part I onto a piece of stiff paper.
4. Wait for the glue to dry. Act cool. You can dance while you wait, too.

PART I
Let it Dry!

5. Cut out Part I (you'll be cutting the stiff paper, too), following Luffy's outline this time. Do it all powerful-like! Carefully cut the slots, following the thick lines around his legs, and make Luffy stand up.

Ta-Da!
Slots

6. Glue Part III and Part IV at right angles to each other, just at the tips!

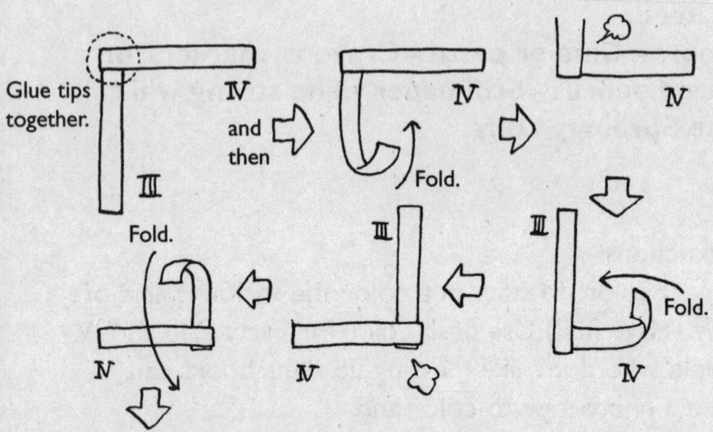
Glue tips together.
IV
III
and then
IV
Fold.
IV
III
Fold.
IV
III
IV
Fold.
IV

And so on and so forth, folding them over and over each other like you're weaving.

← You should get something sproingy like this thing.

↙ Glue the other ends together, and then you're done with this part!

7. Assemble (Rise, Luffy, Rise!)

8. COMPLETION!

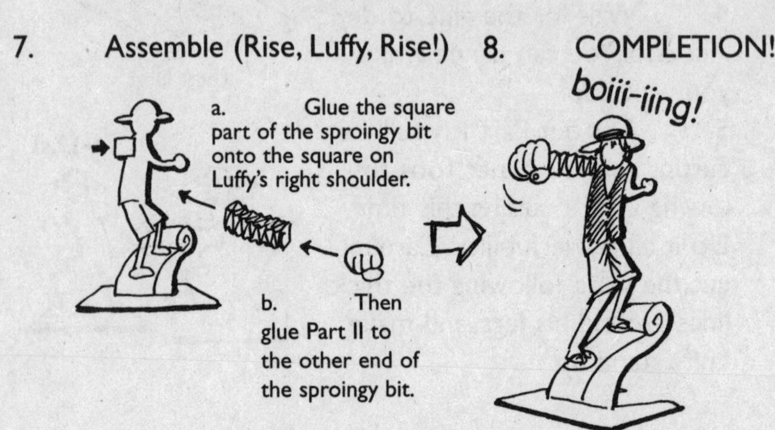
a. Glue the square part of the sproingy bit onto the square on Luffy's right shoulder.
b. Then glue Part II to the other end of the sproingy bit.
boiii-iing!

There's something I'd like to do if I had a whole year off. I would like to do a serious study of different drawing techniques and materials. Then I bet drawing would become even more fun. Whoever said it's a small world?

–Eiichiro Oda, 1998

A SIVE IN
OVA. Ao 1492. a Christophoro
mine regis Castellæ primum detecta.
Noua
Fran-
cia.
Chilaga
Canagadi
Ceuola
Marata
Calicuas
Tagil
Flori-
da.
Cucos
Comos
Culias
Cuchillo
Xalisko
Hispania
noua
Mechula
Trugillo
Granata
Cuba
Jamaica
Caribana
Quito
Ye de los galopegos
TIALIS
Peru.
Lima
Cusco
Insulæ
incognitæ.
AR DEL ZVR.
Amazo
Maragnon fl.
VS CAPRICORNI
EL MAR
PACIFICO.
Cabo de la ysla
Arboledas
Chica
Archipelago
de las islas.

ONE PIECE
Vol. 3
DON'T GET FOOLED AGAIN
Chilaga
Calicuas
Tagil
Marata
STORY AND ART BY
EIICHIRO ODA

MONKEY D. LUFFY
Gifted with rubber powers and bottomless optimism, he's determined to become King of the Pirates.

"RED-HAIRED" SHANKS
A pirate captain who saved young Luffy's life and inspired him with the love of the sea.

THE STORY OF ONE PIECE

· VOLUME 3 ·

Monkey D. Luffy started out as just a kid with a dream—and that dream was to become the greatest pirate in history! Stirred by the tales of pirate "Red-Haired" Shanks, Luffy vowed to become a pirate himself. That was before the enchanted Devil Fruit gave Luffy the power to stretch like rubber, at the cost of being unable to swim—a serious handicap for an aspiring sea dog. Undeterred, Luffy set out to sea, where he found an unlikely partner in the fearsome pirate hunter Roronoa Zolo.

MAYOR BOODLE
The mayor of Port Town, which Buggy and his gang have conquered.

CAPTAIN BUGGY THE CLOWN
Don't let his face fool you—he's bad news.

CHOUCHOU
A dog.

NAMI
A thief who specializes in robbing pirates. The thing she hates most in the world? Pirates!

RORONOA ZOLO
A bounty hunter and master of the "three-sword" fighting style (one in each hand, and one in his mouth!).

Now Luffy and Zolo are under attack by the ruthless pirate lord Buggy the Clown. Captain Buggy has also eaten the Devil Fruit—and gained the power to split his body into pieces like a jigsaw puzzle! How can Luffy fight a foe who's literally all over the place? And can he trust Nami, the fast-talking thief who stole Buggy's ship? As volume 3 of *One Piece* opens, the battle with Buggy is raging... and it's only the beginning of Luffy's problems.

ONE PIECE
ONE PIECE

Vol. 3
DON'T GET FOOLED AGAIN

CONTENTS

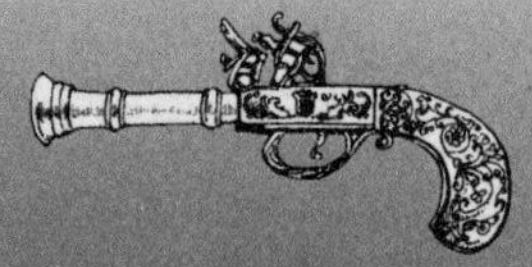

Chapter 18:

THE PIRATE BUGGY THE CLOWN

READ
THIS
WAY

BAM!

WAK!
ZZZ...
ZZZ...

WAK!

KA-BOOM!

RED HAIR!?

YOU TALKIN' ABOUT SHANKS? YOU KNOW SHANKS!?

READ THIS WAY

HMM...
YOU SEEM REAL INTERESTED...
YES, I KNOW HIM. WHAT'S IT TO YOU?

WHERE IS HE NOW?

SO YOU WANT TO KNOW WHERE HE IS, EH? WELL, MAYBE I KNOW...
THEN AGAIN, MAYBE I DON'T.

WHAT ARE YOU TALKING ABOUT?
ARE YOU AN IDIOT?
WATCH YOUR TONGUE, BOY!

WE'RE MORTAL ENEMIES! YOU WON'T GET ANY INFORMATION FROM ME WITHOUT A FIGHT!
NOT EVEN AS A DEPARTING GIFT TO HELL...

WELL, I'M WILLING TO BEAT IT OUT OF YOU.

GA HA HA HA! YOU'LL BE DEAD...
TMP
TMP
BE-FORE YOU GET ONE WORD OUT OF ME!!!

NOT EVEN RUBBER CAN WITH-STAND A RAZOR-SHARP BLADE!
SNIK

MAYBE SO...
GULP

WUP WUP WUP....
CHOP-CHOP...

BUZZ-
SAW!!
SPROING!
!
LET'S
SEE YOU
DODGE
THESE...

READ THIS WAY

WIP
IN MID-AIR!!
WIP WIP
!

N-NO PROBLEM!
WOING
WUP

FWISH FWISH!
FWUP!

READ THIS WAY

HA!!

NOT BAD! THIS IS GETTING INTER-ESTING!

FWUP

SURE IS!

SNAP!

GUM-GUM...

PISTOL!!!

!

INTEREST-ING POWER YOU'VE GOT THERE!

READ THIS WAY

BUT YOUR OUT-STRETCHED ARM...

...MAKES A DELICIOUS TARGET!

WAP!

I'LL JUST SEVER IT!!

REEEENG

HUH!?

GUM-GUM...

READ THIS WAY
CHOP-CHOP QUICK DODGE!!
VOING
...SICKLE!!
OOSH!!
POP!

READ THIS WAY

KRASH
GA HA HA HA HA!

YOU UNDER-ESTIMATE ME, GUMMY BOY!!
WAP

UMF!!
KRASH

READ THIS WAY

DARN...
HOW AM I SUPPOSED TO WHACK YOU WHEN YOU KEEP FLYING TO PIECES?
WUP
KLAK
KLAK

...!!

WHAT A FIGHT!
IT'S LIKE I'M SEEING THINGS...

DID YA SEE THAT?
QUIET, FOOL! WE'RE SUPPOSED TO BE UNCONSCIOUS!!

IF WE GET MIXED UP IN A FIGHT LIKE THIS...
...WE'RE MINCEMEAT!!

READ THIS WAY
FOOM
CHOP-CHOP HARPOON!!!
WOOSH
!
URK!!!
SW
AP!
SLISH
!
SEPARATE!
AGH!

READ
THIS
WAY

!
KRASH

...
?

WOOOOO
PLIP
PLIP

DARN YOU!

WHATSA MATTER? BABY GET A BOO BOO?

THAT DOES IT!!
PLIP PLIP
YOU NICKED MY HAT!!!

READ THIS WAY

SO?

THIS IS MY TREASURE!!!

NOBODY DAMAGES THIS HAT!!!

!

MY FRIEND GAVE ME THIS HAT A LONG TIME AGO.

I THOUGHT NOTHING FAZED THIS GUY...
BUT HE LOOKS PRETTY MAD.
...

...
IT'S THAT IMPORT-ANT TO YOU, EH?

THAT'S RIGHT!!
FWUP

READ THIS WAY

WOOSH

YOW!

FWOOSH

!?

THEN YOU SHOULD TAKE BETTER CARE OF IT!!!

SHUK
!!!!
DO ME A FAVOR...
KEEP THIS HAT SAFE FOR ME?

....!!
HAHAHAHAHAHA
GRRR!!

GA HA HA HA HA! YOU CALL THIS BEAT-UP OLD THING YOUR TREASURE!?
GA HA HA HA HA HA
WUP!

THIS HAT MEANS A LOT TO ME.
HA HA
HA HA
PROMISE THAT YOU'LL GIVE IT BACK TO ME SOMEDAY...

...WHEN YOU'VE BECOME A GREAT PIRATE.
TUMP
I PROMISED I'D RETURN THAT HAT TO SHANKS!

WHAT?
THIS IS SHANKS'S HAT?
FWUP
I THOUGHT IT LOOKED FAMILIAR...

SHANKS AND I WORKED ON THE SAME PIRATE SHIP A LONG TIME AGO.
PTU
WE WERE BOTH YOUNG...
SPLAT
APPRENTICE PIRATES, YOU MIGHT SAY...
!!

SHANKS IS A GREAT MAN!
WOING
!
APPREN-TICE PIRATES... TOGETHER?
CHOP-CHOP QUICK ESCAPE!!
SPOINK!

!!!?
DON'T PUT YOURSELF ON THE SAME LEVEL AS HIM!!!
...!!!

Early Sketch: Boogie the Clown!

ROMANCE
DAWN

Chapter 19:

DEVIL FRUIT

DANGER

FWUMP
ARG!!!

WAP
...!!!

READ THIS WAY

DARN YOU! YOU RUINED MY HAT!!
ARGH! KOF KOF!

AND YOU SPAT ON IT!!
YECH! STHOP IT!
HERF HERF HERF
IT'S YOUR OWN SPIT!!

WUK WUK WUK!!
DON'T EVER MENTION SHANKS AND YOURSELF...
OWIE OWIE!
...IN THE SAME BREATH AGAIN!

WUK WUK
HMPH! I DON'T KNOW WHAT YOUR CONNECTION TO SHANKS IS...
BUT I'LL SAY WHATEVER I LIKE ABOUT HIM!!
OH YEAH?
CHOP-CHOP...
!

DON'T COME APART!!

UNGH!!!

HEY...
THE CAPTAIN'S NOT LOSING, IS HE?
OF COURSE NOT!

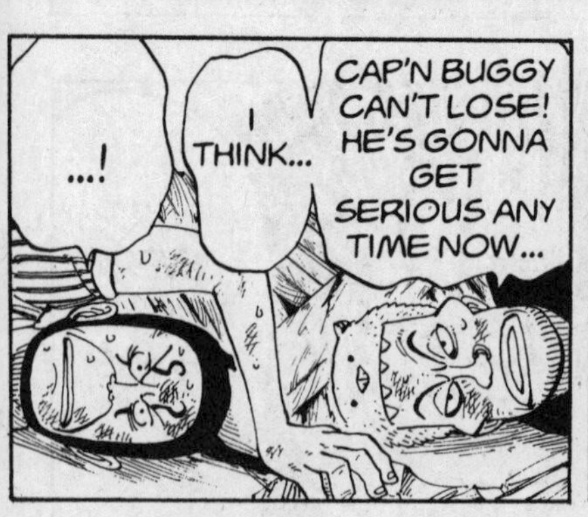
CAP'N BUGGY CAN'T LOSE! HE'S GONNA GET SERIOUS ANY TIME NOW...
I THINK...
...!

...!

GASP!
OH NO! I GOT CAUGHT UP WATCHING THE FIGHT!
I HAVE TO STEAL THE TREASURE AND MAKE MY ESCAPE!

THE CAMP OF THE TOWNS-PEOPLE
SOME-THING'S WRONG.
SIGH
SIGH
THE MAYOR'S BEEN GONE TOO LONG.
...

BLAST 'IM!
HE'S WORRYING EVERYONE.

MAYBE SOMETHING HAPPENED IN TOWN!
YEAH! WE'VE HEARD A LOT OF CANNON FIRE TODAY...
BLAB
BLAB

OKAY...
TA-
DUM
I'M GOING INTO TOWN.
THE REST OF YOU, STAY HERE!
!

READ THIS WAY

DON'T BE A FOOL! THOSE AREN'T JUST ANY PIRATES!
THEY'RE BUGGY'S INFAMOUS PIRATE CREW!

I WON'T LET YOU GO ALONE!
I'M GOING WITH YOU!

THAT'S WHY WE'RE GOING WITH YOU!!
YEAH!!
!
WE CAN'T CALL OURSELVES GOOD CITIZENS...
IF WE DON'T DEFEND OUR MAYOR!

AND YOU CAN'T STOP US.
WE'RE DOING THIS OF OUR OWN FREE WILL!
...!

...
DO WHAT YOU WANT, THEN!
LET'S GO, EVERY-BODY!!
YEAH!!

READ THIS WAY

NEVER IN MY LIFE...
HAS ANYONE MADE ME AS ANGRY AS SHANKS DID!!

THAT SCALAWAG...
...STOLE A GREAT TREASURE FROM ME!!!

!
I'LL NEVER FORGIVE HIM FOR THAT!!
HEY! THEY'RE FIGHTING AGAIN!
HAR HAR HAR! GO TO IT!! FIGHT IT OUT!
YAR
HAR

IT'S THE NORTH POLE!
NO, THE SOUTH POLE!!
YOU'RE A STUB-BORN FOOL!!
I'M STUBBORN 'CAUSE I KNOW I'M RIGHT!!
YAR
ARG
BIFF!
BONK!
POW!
THAT'S ENOUGH!
YOU TWO ARE ALWAYS FIGHTING!
BONK
BONK
URF!
OOF!
WHO CARES WHETHER IT'S COLDER AT THE SOUTH POLE OR THE NORTH POLE?
HA HA HA HA HA HA
...
IF YOU MUST KNOW, THEN GO FIND OUT FOR YOURSELVES!
YOU TWO NEED TO COOL OFF!

SHIP APPROACHING!! NORTH BY NORTHEAST!!
HEAD STRAIGHT FOR 'EM!!
YARR!
IT'S TIME TO FIGHT!
YOU LOOK HAPPY, BUGGY.
OF COURSE I'M HAPPY! A SHIP IS TREASURE FOR THE TAKING!
HMMM... MAYBE YOU'RE RIGHT.
MAYBE!? MAYBE I'M RIGHT!? I'M ABSOLUTELY RIGHT!!
SHIK
YOU'RE SOFT! YOU AND ALL THE PIRATES ON THIS SHIP!
NONE OF YOU HAS A PROPER APPRECIATION FOR BOOTY!!
YOU'VE LOST SIGHT OF WHAT BEING A PIRATE IS ALL ABOUT!!

YAY!!
YARR!!
ARG!
KLANG
KLANK!
YAAAAHHH!
YARR!
UNGH!!
HUH!?
FWIP
WHAT'S THIS?
A MAP TO A VAST FORTUNE SUNKEN DEEP ON THE OCEAN FLOOR!
T- T- TREA--
WHAM!
TREASURE MAP!!!
I COULDN'T STOP SHAKING!
MY FIRST TREASURE MAP!

N-NOBODY'S LOOKING...
HA HA HA! MAYBE I'LL JUST KEEP THIS TO MYSELF!
RWIP
IT'S MINE! I DID IT!
MY
ORTUNE
IS AS
OOD AS
ADE!!!
HA HA HA HA HA!!
ANOTHER VICTORY!!
DA HA HA HA HA HA HA HA
DRINK! SING! MAKE MERRY!
HEY, BUGGY! COME JOIN THE FUN! LOOK AT OUR SPOILS! WE GOT SOMETHING REAL INTERESTING!!
!
SLAM
HA HA HA HA
S-S-SPOILS? I... UH... DIDN'T TAKE ANYTHING...
I DON'T KNOW ANYTHING ABOUT IT!!
?
WHAT'RE YOU TALKING ABOUT?

I SUPPOSE SOMEDAY
WE'LL LEAVE THIS SHIP.
SWUMP
AYE... I'LL GO OFF ON MY OWN SOMEDAY...
AS CAPTAIN OF MY OWN SHIP!
I'LL MAKE TIME TO SEE THE WORLD.
I'LL DO SOME PIRATING ALONG THE WAY, OF COURSE.
HEH HEH! STILL A SOFT FOOL.
WHAT?
BUT YOU'RE A GOOD FIGHTER, I'LL GIVE YOU THAT.
IF IT WEREN'T FOR YOUR SOFT WAY OF THINKING, I'D ASK YOU TO BE ON MY CREW.

WORK FOR YOU? NEVER!
FWIP
WE THINK DIFFERENTLY! BETTER IF WE GO OUR SEPARATE WAYS...
BEING A PIRATE IS ALL ABOUT GOING YOUR OWN WAY.
HA HA HA HA!!
HOW WOULD YOU KNOW WHAT BEING A PIRATE IS ABOUT?
IF EVER WE CROSS PATHS ON THE HIGH SEAS, IT'LL BE A FIGHT TO THE FINISH! AGREED?
AGREED.
THAT'S ALSO WHAT BEING A PIRATE IS ALL ABOUT.
PON
SOMETIMES, YOU BAFFLE ME...
HMPH
NOW WHAT WERE YOU YAMMERING ABOUT? SOMETHING INTERESTING?
AYE... WE FOUND SOME DEVIL FRUIT.

THEY SAY THAT THE DEVIL FRUIT WAS ENCHANTED BY SEA DEVILS.
WHOEVER EATS IT GETS AMAZING POWERS, BUT THE SEAS TURN AGAINST THEM...
CAP'N SAYS ANYONE WHO WANTS TO CAN EAT IT.
GA HA HA HA! WHAT SEADOG WOULD GIVE UP HIS ABILITY TO SWIM?
HMPH! ONLY A FOOL WOULD EAT THAT FRUIT!
KRCH
THERE'S TONS OF TREASURE ON THE OCEAN FLOOR. YOU CAN'T GET IT IF YOU CAN'T SWIM.
THAT DEVIL FRUIT'S WORTH A FORTUNE, YOU KNOW...
SOME PEOPLE WILL PAY 100 MILLION BERRIES FOR IT.
IMPOSSIBLE!
SPROING!!
100 MILLION BERRIES!? A DOZEN TREASURE CHESTS WOULDN'T HOLD IT ALL!! THE GODDESS OF TREASURE MUST BE SMILING ON ME!!

I, APPRENTICE PIRATE BUGGY...
TA-DA!
WILL EAT THE DEVIL FRUIT!!

AH HA HA HA HA! YOUNGSTERS DON'T THINK ABOUT CONSEQUENCES!
AYE, BUT BUGGY'S GOT REAL SAND IN HIS CRAW!
ULP!
ARR! HE ATE IT!!!

OOOO
WELL? FEEL ANY DIFFERENT?
NOT REALLY.

HMPH! MAYBE IT WASN'T RIPE...
MAYBE THOSE TALES ABOUT THE DEVIL FRUIT WERE LIES!

HEH HEH HEH!! THEY FELL FOR IT! THE FRUIT I JUST ATE WAS FAKE! I SWITCHED IT WITH THE REAL DEVIL FRUIT LAST NIGHT!

HA HA HA HA HA
ANOTHER GLORIOUS SUCCESS!!
NO MORE APPRENTICING! I'M GETTING OFF THIS HULK BEFORE SOMEONE FINDS ME OUT!!
WITH THE DEVIL FRUIT AND THE TREASURE MAP, I'LL SOON BE RICH!
I'LL PUT TOGETHER THE CRUELEST PIRATE CREW EVER AND STEAL MORE TREASURE!
WHATCHA DOING, BUGGY?
HERK!!
URP
FIP
WHAT'S WRONG WITH YOUR FACE?
?
PHEW! IT'S ONLY SHANKS!
STOP STEAL-ING FOOD!
THE COOK'LL SKIN YOU ALIVE.
TMP TMP
THAT WAS CLOSE ...
OH! I ALMOST FORGOT! THE CAPTAIN SAID –
YIKES!
GULP!!

AAAAAAAAAAAH!!
AAAAAAA
FWP
!?
Y-Y-YOU!!!! I... I--!!!
AAAAAAAAAAH!!
HEY! YOU DROPPED SOME-THING!
FLIT
AAAAAAA
AAAAAGH! MY MAP!!!
FLIT
SPLOOSH
HEY, BUGGY!!
!!?
WHAT'S HAPPEN-ING!? I CAN'T MOVE RIGHT!
GLUG
GLUG

PLASH PLASH
GASP!... BLUB... GLUG...!!!
HELP!!!
PLASH
YOU'RE SUP-POSED TO BE A GREAT SWIMMER!!
SHANKS! WHAT'S GOING ON?
WHAT'S HE DOING DOWN THERE?

HOLD ON! I'M COMING!!
SHANKS!!
I SWALLOWED A HUNDRED MILLION BERRIES! NOW I CAN'T SWIM, SO I CAN'T GET AT THAT TREASURE ON THE OCEAN FLOOR!

HMMM... SO SHANKS SAVED YOUR LIFE!
SO WHAT!!?
IP!!
IT WAS ALL HIS FAULT! HE FOILED ALL MY GRANDIOSE PLANS!!!

SO I CHANGED MY PLANS. IF I CAN'T GET TREASURE THAT'S *IN* THE SEA, I'LL JUST HAVE TO TAKE ALL THE TREASURE *ON* THE SEA–
USING MY CHOP-CHOP POWER!
!

I DON'T CARE HOW INSIGNIFICANT A FLY YOU MIGHT BE...
IF YOU PUT YOUR HANDS ON MY TREASURE...
UH-OH...
FWOOSH
I'LL SQUASH YOU!!!
HUH?

Buggy the Pirate His Evolution

Part 1

Die gloriously!

✣ About "Boogie" and Gang...

Some of you may be wondering who this "Boogie" is. That was my original name for Captain Buggy.

✣ Why did he become "Buggy"?

One day I saw a movie with a character named "Boogie." I thought, "Darn, Boogie's already taken. Oh well, I'll name him Buggy!" (Total thinking time: 0.2 seconds.)

✣ Why does Buggy have a big round nose?

So he'll look like a clown, of course.

✣ Who's the guy on the far left of the Boogie sketch?

Hmm... who is that guy on the far left? Back then, none of the three pirates behind Boogie had names. All I really had in mind was that the crew should include a strongman, an animal trainer, and some kind of strange swordsman. The sketch shows them at a stage when they were still very far from completion.

Chapter 20:

THE WAY OF THE THIEF

HANDS OFF MY TREASURE!!
FA-WOOSH
!
I'LL CUT YOU TO PIECES!!
YOU WON'T GET THE BETTER OF ME, NAMI!!!
I'VE BEEN FOUND OUT!

READ THIS WAY

...
WOOSH
KYAAAA!!!
HUFF HUFF!!
YOU WON'T EVEN GET A SPECK OF GOLD PAINT!

AAGH!!!
THWMP

HUH?

FUMP

!

ARRGH!!!

TWITCH TWITCH
C-CURSE YOU... GUM-GUM BOY!
YOU FIGHT DIRTY... ATTACKING MY LOWER HALF...!!!

DON'T FOR-GET...
OUR FIGHT'S NOT OVER!
FLIP FLOP
FWUP
CHIKA

I'M SAFE...
PHEW

HEY! DROP THE LOOT AND GET OUTTA HERE!
!
HE'LL KEEP COMING AFTER YOU!!

LEAVE THE TREASURE!? NOT A CHANCE!!
I'M NOT GONNA LEAVE MY TREASURE BEHIND!

"YOUR" TREASURE!?

THAT'S RIGHT! MY TREASURE! I'M A MASTER THIEF, AND I JUST STOLE IT!!
MINE, MINE, MINE!!!

OH...
HMPH!
PWIP!
OKAY...

READ THIS WAY

THAT'S MY TREASURE, FOOL!! IT'S NOT YOURS UNTIL YOU GET AWAY WITH IT!!
IT'S A BASIC TENET OF THIEVERY!

THE BAD GUY WANTS TO LECTURE THE BAD GUY, EH?
I DON'T ARGUE WITH LOWLIFE PIRATES!
WHAT!?

I'D NEVER STOOP SO LOW...

...AS TO TAKE LESSONS FROM YOU!!

READ THIS WAY

CHOMP
THEN SUFFER THE CONSE-QUENCES!!

CHOP-CHOP...
......!!
CHIKA

OOF!

...FESTIVAL!!!

BOO-M

OOF!

DARN! HE'S ALL OVER THE PLACE!!
WOOSH
HOW AM I SUPPOSED TO FIGHT HIM?
AH HA HA HA!! LET'S SEE YOU SAVE YOUR FRIEND NOW, GUM-GUM BOY!!!
WOOSH
WOOSH

GIVE IT BACK!!
GIMME BACK MY TREASURE!!
TMP TMP TMP TMP

HUH?
TUP TUP TUP
HIS FEET DON'T FLY...

I GOT YOUR FOOT!!
AHA!!

KOOCHIE KOOCHIE

KOOCHIE!

HUH?

URK...!!

HOW DO YOU LIKE THIS!?

YAAAHH!!

BAH HA HA HA HA HA HA HA HA! ST-STOP!

YOU'RE A TOUGH OLD CLOWN, AREN'T YA?

YAAHHH!

OUCH!!

URGH!!

ENOUGH ALREADY!! CUT IT OUT!!!
FWIP
...
THE ONE WHO'S GONNA CUT IT OUT...
SKRUF SKRUF
HUF
HUF
...!!
!

IS YOU!

HEH...

WOW!!

READ
THIS
WAY

THANK YOU...
FOR RETURNING MY TREASURE!!
!

...!!
TUG
LET GO...!!!
TUG

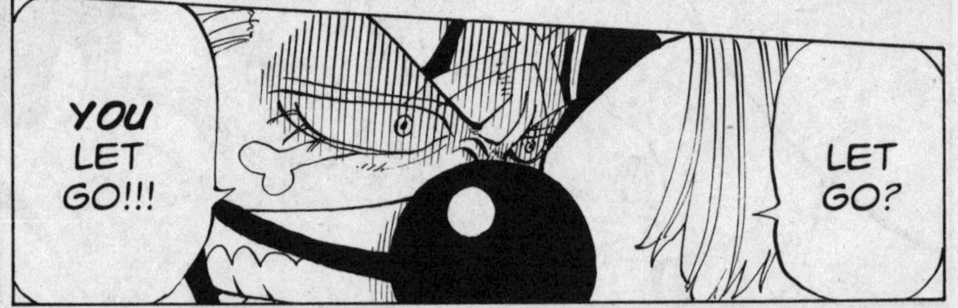
LET GO?
YOU LET GO!!!

READ
THIS
WAY

TUP TUP TUP TUP
TUP TUP TUP!!
WOOO!!
IT'S MY TREASURE!!!
!?

WOOSH!!
HEY! YOU'RE SUPPOSED TO BE FIGHTING ME!
HUH?

URF!!!
REMEMBER?
!

KRASH

SHAOOO

GOTCHA!

...

FUP FUP

FUP

READ THIS WAY

SWF

THAT...

...WAS FOR THE MAYOR!!

CHING!

...
HUF HUF

THANKS FOR SAVING ME.
NO PROBLEM!

HEY! THE TREASURE MAP!
MY TREASURE'S SCATTERED ALL OVER THE PLACE!!

BAM!
AT LAST!!
IT'S THE MAP OF THE GRAND LINE!!

HEY...
WOOO
NOT SO FAST, GUM-GUM BOY!!
!
!

HMPH! YOU STILL ALIVE?
HUF
HUF
I'LL KILL YOU!!
COME TO-GETHER!
CHOP-CHOP...

HUH!?

IS THIS...
WHAT YOU'RE LOOKING FOR?

AGH!! MY BODY!!

HA HA HA HA!
GOOD JOB, MASTER THIEF!
LEAVE THE REST TO ME!

GOOD-BYE, BUGGY!!
WOING
GUM-GUM...
WAIT!!
BAZOOKA !!!!
AAAA!!!
AAAAAAAH

One Piece Storyboards #6

海賊王になる
…!!!
プル…
プル
ハデアホがァ!!!
フザけんなァ!!!
てめェが海賊王だと!? ならば
おれァ神か!!? 世界の宝を
手にするのはこのおれだ!!!
夢みてんじゃねェ!!!

Chapter 21:

TOWNIES

BA-M
I WIN!!

NOW YOU'LL JOIN MY CREW, RIGHT?

FOR THE TIME BEING.

LOOKS LIKE I'LL MAKE A FORTUNE IF I STICK WITH YOU GUYS.

ERK
YOU HAVE TO GIVE BUGGY CREDIT-- HE HAD AN EYE FOR TREASURE. THIS IS FIRST-CLASS BOOTY.
IT'S EASILY WORTH 10 MILLION BERRIES.
CHING

TA—DA!

HEY, ALL THIS TREASURE WEIGHS A TON, SO I DIVIDED IT IN TWO. YOU CARRY HALF, OKAY?

THAT HAT MEANS A LOT TO YOU, HUH?
...

!

FWUMP!
YEAH. IT'S NOT SO BAD, I GUESS. I CAN STILL WEAR IT.
IT SURE FELT GOOD TO CLOBBER OL' BUGGY!!

READ THIS WAY

HEAR THAT? CAP'N BUGGY GOT CLOB-BERED!
W-WHAT SHOULD WE DO?

I THINK I'LL PLAY DEAD A WHILE LONGER.
GOOD IDEA.
FWUMP!

HEY, ZOLO! WAKE UP!
LET'S GET GOING!
PAT PAT
HUH?

...!
DID YOU TAKE CARE OF THINGS?
YEAH, AND I GOT THE MAP AND THE TREASURE.
WAAAH

UNGH! IT'S NO GOOD. I DON'T THINK I CAN WALK.
OOOG
OF COURSE NOT! IF YOU COULD, I WOULDN'T BELIEVE EITHER OF YOU GUYS ARE HUMAN.

HEY! DON'T LUMP ME WITH HIM!
YOU'RE EVEN LESS HUMAN THAN HE IS!

OH, YEAH!
ZZZZZ
I'D BETTER WAKE THE MAYOR!

HEY, YOU GUYS...
TMP
!

WE'RE THE CITIZENS OF THIS TOWN.
GRRR...
DID THE PIRATES MUTINY OR SOMETHING? C'MON, YOU, TALK!

THE TOWNS-PEOPLE? THAT'S A RELIEF!
PHEW!
THOUGHT YOU MIGHT BE MORE PIRATES.

WE'LL TELL YOU WHAT HAPPENED, BUT IT'S A LONG STORY...
HEY! IT'S THE MAYOR!!

MAYOR! ARE YOU HURT?
WHAT HAPPENED HERE?
IT WAS THOSE LOUSY PIRATES!

TA--DA!
NO, IT WASN'T...
I KNOCKED THE OLD MAN OUT!
!

VEEEM!!
HUH!?

LUFFY! THEY DIDN'T HAVE TO KNOW THAT!!
WELL, YOU SAW ME.
TRUE, BUT I WASN'T GOING TO TELL THEM!

THEY'RE IN AN UGLY MOOD.
DON'T TELL THEM WE'RE PIRATES AND THIEVES, OR THEY'LL KILL US!!

YOU DID THIS TO THE MAYOR!?
IT'S INTOLER-ABLE!
WHO ARE YOU? PIRATES?
!

BA-DA——DUM
WE'RE PIRATES!!
!!!

WIP
PIRATES!! GET 'EM!!
WIP

HA HA HA

YOU IDIOT!
WE *ARE* PIRATES!

RUN!!
TMP TMP
THEY'RE RUNNING!!
AFTER THEM!!
AAGH!!

DON'T LET 'EM GET AWAY!!
THEY'LL PAY FOR ATTACKING THE MAYOR!!

WHY DO YOU ALWAYS HAVE TO COMPLICATE THINGS?
THESE ARE GOOD PEOPLE!

SO!?

RAARR
THEY'RE ALL WORKED UP...
BECAUSE THEY LOVE THEIR MAYOR!

IT WOULDN'T MATTER WHAT WE TOLD THEM!
RAARR
...!

THEY'RE GOING INTO THAT ALLEY!!
WIP!

RRRR!!!

YIKES!
EEEK

CHOU-CHOU!
IT'S THAT DOG!

GET OUT OF THE WAY, CHOU-CHOU!!
THOSE GUYS ARE **BAD** PEOPLE!
GRRR... WOOF!

GRRRR...!!

WOOF!! WOOF!!
CHOU-CHOU! WHY ARE YOU HELPING THEM!?
WOOF!!

CHOU-CHOU!
GET OUT OF THE WAY!!
WOOF!! WOOF!!

...

PHEW! THAT WAS TOO CLOSE! CHOUCHOU REALLY SAVED OUR NECKS!
WHY ARE WE IN THIS MESS, ANYWAY?
IT'S OKAY. WE DID WHAT WE NEEDED TO DO, RIGHT?
I GUESS SO...

HEY, IS THIS YOUR SHIP?

TA—DA
IT'S GREAT!!!
I'VE SEEN BETTER...
I STOLE IT FROM SOME STUPID PIRATES.

HUH?
TOMP!!
HUH?
WE'VE BEEN WAITING FOR YOU, GIRLIE!!

Y-YOU GUYS...

WE KNEW YOU'D COME BACK TO THE SHIP!

HAR HAR HAR HAR! IMAGINE OUR SURPRISE, FINDING OUR STOLEN SHIP DOCKED HERE!

YOU HAVEN'T FORGOTTEN ABOUT US, HAVE YOU?

TA-DA!

FRIENDS OF YOURS?
NOT SO MUCH...
NOW, THAT'S NOT NICE. OUR FATES ARE INTER-TWINED.

I SEE YOU BROUGHT SOME FRIENDS...
THEN THEY'LL GET THE SAME TREATMENT AS YOU!
WE'LL LEARN YE TO STEAL SHIPS!
WHAT AILS YE?
LOOK AT ME WHEN I'M TALKING TO YOU!
WAP
WAP

OW.

!!!?

YAAAAH!!
TMP TMP TMP
HUH!?
TMP TMP-TMP-TMP TMP

THE MAYOR! HE'S COMING AROUND!
PHEW! THANK GOOD-NESS!!
NNGH ...!!
MAYOR! WHAT HAPPENED?

OOOO
WHAT THE--?
IT WAS LIKE THIS WHEN WE GOT HERE...
DON'T YOU KNOW WHAT HAPPENED?

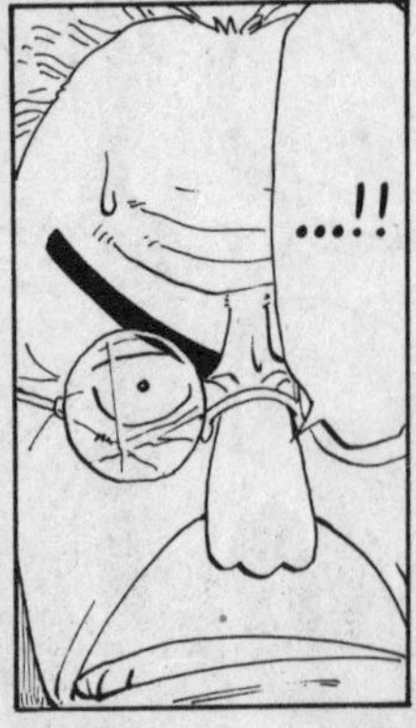
...!!

THERE WERE THREE SUSPICIOUS CHARACTERS HERE...
THE KID AND HIS FRIENDS!
THEN THEY'RE... STILL ALIVE?

WE'LL TEACH THOSE PIRATES TO RESPECT DECENT CITIZENS!
BUT WE'D LIKE TO GET OUR HANDS ON 'EM! HE WAS MOCKING US!!
WE JUST CHASED THAT PIRATE AND HIS FRIENDS OUT OF TOWN!!
BOOKS

FWAK!
THAT BLASTED KID! HOW COULD HE HAVE DONE THAT TO AN OLD MAN LIKE ME?

LET'S GET THOSE SCOUN-DRELS!!
SHUT UP!!!
!

I'M THE ONLY ONE WHO GETS TO CALL THEM NAMES!!
DON'T ANY OF YOU DARE TALK BAD ABOUT THEM!!!

B-BUT MAYOR... WHY ARE YOU STICKING UP FOR PIRATES?
THAT DERN KID! DOES HE THINK HE CAN GET AWAY WITHOUT HEARING FROM ME?

READ THIS WAY

WHERE'D THEY GO? WHICH WAY?
UH... THEY RAN FOR THE DOCKS!
KLINK KLINK

TUMP TUMP!!
MAYOR!!!

THE NERVE OF THAT KID! THIS IS MY TOWN!
KLANK
WOOSH
TON TON
I'VE GOT A THING OR TWO TO SAY TO HIM!!
KLATTER

FWAP
ALL RIGHT! LET'S GO!
FWAP

HEY! YOUR SAIL HAS BUGGY'S MARK ON IT!
IT WAS HIS SHIP! I'LL REPLACE IT LATER.

HUFF
HEY, KID! WAIT!
HUFF

I HAVE SOMETHING TO SAY TO YOU!
THE MAYOR!

I WAS A DESPERATE MAN!
BUGGY WOULD HAVE KILLED ME! YOU SAVED ME AND MY TOWN!
HUFF
HUFF

THANK YOU!
I WON'T FORGET IT!!
YOU'RE WELCOME, MAYOR!
TAKE IT EASY!
!
WORDS CAN'T EX-PRESS...

WHAT!? YOU LEFT THE TREASURE!?
THAT WAS HALF A MILLION BERRIES I HANDED YOU!!
YEAH, BUT THEIR WHOLE TOWN WAS WRECKED. THEY'LL NEED A LOT OF MONEY TO REBUILD IT.
THAT WAS MY TREASURE YOU GAVE AWAY!

TAKE IT EASY! IF YOU REALLY WANT IT, LET'S GO BACK AND GET IT!
AAAAH!
IT'S TOO LATE! IF YOU EVER DO ANYTHING LIKE THAT AGAIN, I'LL KILL YOU!
HA HA HA HA HA HA HA!

AND SO NAMI THE THIEF JOINS LUFFY'S CREW, AND THE TWO SHIPS SET OUT TO SEA TOGETHER.
IDIOT!
YOU'RE LAUGHING!
HEE HEE. NO I'M NOT!!
WHAK!
THAT DIDN'T HURT.
LITTLE DO THEY KNOW THAT SOON THEY'LL HAVE TO FACE THE TRIAL OF THE FOREST...

One Piece Storyboards #7

嗚呼 今日も…
ザザーン
あっちの海から朗らかな一日が始まる!!
村の若者 ウソップ
チュン
チュン…

Chapter 22:
STRANGE CREATURES

SKREE
SKREE

TMP

YOU FIXED IT!!!

IT'S A TEMPORARY FIX.
I JUST SEWED UP THE HOLES...

IT'LL BE FINE IF YOU AREN'T TOO ROUGH WITH IT.
THANKS!! THAT HAT WAS FULL OF HOLES...
AND NOW YOU CAN'T EVEN TELL!
POKE
POKE
POKE

IT'S ALL-
!
POP
OOPS!

YOU DON'T LISTEN!!
YEEOW!
BUSU!!

YOU STABBED ME WITH THAT NEEDLE!
WELL, THAT'S THE ONLY WAY I CAN HURT YOU!

HMM... YOU'RE RIGHT!
CUT THE RACKET! I CAN'T SLEEP.
AND I'M STARVING.

HEY, SHARE SOME OF YOUR RATIONS WITH US!
WHAT'S WRONG WITH YOU GUYS?
DON'T YOU KNOW ANYTHING ABOUT SEAMANSHIP? YOU DON'T EVEN HAVE ANY FOOD OR WATER!
YOU HAVE TO RESPECT THE SEA!
HEY! I SEE SOME-THING!

HOW HAVE YOU LUNK-HEADS SURVIVED THIS LONG?
WE MANAGE.
HEY! IT'S AN ISLAND!
FORGET IT...
IT LOOKS UNINHABITED. HOLD YOUR COURSE...

DOOM
COME BACK!!!
KREEK
KREEK
MAYBE THERE'S SOMEONE THERE WHO WILL JOIN OUR CREW!
MAYBE YOU CAN FIND SOME FOOD. BUT NAMI'S RIGHT. WE'RE NOT PREPARED.

WE'VE FOUND A DESERTED ISLAND!
OOOOO
LOOKS LIKE THERE'S NOTHING HERE BUT TREES!
I TOLD YOU IT WAS UNINHAB-ITED.
YOU WON'T FIND ANYONE TO JOIN YOUR CREW HERE.
HEY, ZOLO! GET OVER HERE!
DON

READ THIS WAY

HONK
HONK
HE'S ASLEEP!
HMPH!
LET HIM REST. HE'S STILL RECOVERING FROM HIS INJURIES.

GOOD THINKING! OKAY, LET'S GO!
GO WHERE!?

MAYBE THERE ARE PEOPLE LIVING DEEP IN THE FOREST.
PEOPLE, NO. HUNGRY MONSTERS, MAYBE.

KLUCK KLUCK KLUCK
HUH?
HUH?
TMP TMP ...
CLUCK
CLUCK

WHAT IS THAT!?
KLUCK
TMP
TMP

HEY, LOOK!
IT'S SOME KIND OF WEIRD RABBIT!
SSSSS
YEAH, WEIRD IS RIGHT.
BUT MORE LIKE A WEIRD SNAKE THAN A RABBIT!

AND LOOK AT THAT LION!
SHUF SHUF
LION!? THAT'S SOME STRANGE BREED OF PIG!
GRUNT GRUNT

THERE'S SOME-THING ODD ABOUT THIS FOREST.

DO NOT COME ANY FURTHER!!
HUH?

WHO SAID THAT?
WHO ARE YOU?
I... AM THE GUARDIAN OF THE FOREST!!
HUH?

THE GUARDIAN OF THE FOREST?
THAT'S RIGHT! IF YOU VALUE YOUR LIVES, YOU'LL LEAVE THIS PLACE NOW!
...

ARE YOU PIRATES?
THAT'S RIGHT.
WHY WOULD HE ASK US THAT?
SO YOU **ARE** PIRATES!

DON'T YOU DARE TAKE ANOTHER STEP INTO THIS FOREST!
IF YOU DO, YOU MUST FACE THE TRIAL OF THE FOREST. WILL YOU RISK HAVING YOUR BODIES DISMEMBERED?
WHO CARES?
WHY'RE YOU ASKING ME ALL THIS STUFF?
WHAT'S HE TALKING ABOUT?

I THINK SOMETHING'S WRONG WITH HIM.
WHAT DID YOU SAY, YOU STRAW-HATTED FOOL!?
WHERE ARE YOU? SHOW YOURSELF!
I THINK HE'S OVER THERE...
I WARNED YOU NOT TO COME ANY CLOSER!
SHUF
SHUF
NOW YOU MUST FACE THE TRIAL OF THE FOREST!
?
HUH?

HUMF!

BAM

AAAH!!

WOING

FWOOM

OOF!!

!!

...!!!?
...HUH...!?

TH-THAT REALLY SCARED ME! WAS THAT A GUN?
WOW. EVEN BULLETS CAN'T HURT YOU!

WHEW

NO, BUT THEY SCARE ME, TOO, SO I DON'T LIKE BEING SHOT!

WHAT...
WHAT ARE YOU?
WHAT ARE YOU?

THE BULLET CAME FROM OVER HERE!
!
LOOK! THERE'S A PISTOL ON THE GROUND!

WHAT'S THIS?
IT LOOKS REAL SUSPICIOUS!
...
HUH——?

TUMP TUMP
HEY! IT'S MOVING!

UNGH!!
...
PWUMP

DOON
HEY! HELP ME UP!!

I-IT'S A PERSON...
HELP ME UP, I SAID!
HE LOOKS LIKE A SHRUB!
TWITCH
WIGGLE
HE TRIPPED HIMSELF, AND NOW HE'S ACTING INDIGNANT.

THE FRUIT OF THE GUM-GUM TREE...
THE DEVIL FRUIT, EH?
I'VE HEARD THE TALES...
BUT THIS IS THE FIRST TIME I'VE EVER MET SOMEONE WHO'S EATEN THE FRUIT.
DA
GAIMON KEEPER OF THE ISLAND
AND THIS IS THE FIRST TIME I'VE EVER SEEN A GUY STUCK IN A TREASURE CHEST!
ARE YOU A "BOXER"?
WELL, WHEN I WAS YOUNG-ER...
HEY! THAT'S A STUPID JOKE!
I'M STUCK AND I CAN'T GET OUT!!
YOU CAN'T IMAGINE HOW MISER-ABLE I'VE BEEN!!
I'VE BEEN ALONE ON THIS ISLAND FOR 20 YEARS!!!
TWENTY YEARS!?
YOU'VE BEEN ALL ALONE?
THAT'S RIGHT. TWENTY YEARS...

YOU MUST BE STUPID!
I'LL MURDER YA!!!
HYAAAH!
...
TWENTY YEARS... IT'S BEEN A LONG TIME...
THAT'S WHY MY HAIR AND BEARD ARE THIS LONG.
AND I USED TO HAVE **TWO** EYE-BROWS!

I HAVEN'T HAD A CONVERSATION WITH ANOTHER PERSON IN ALL THAT TIME!

OW! OUCH! WHAT'RE YOU DOING!?
YANK YANK
YOU'RE STUCK!
CUT IT OUT! YOU'LL BREAK MY NECK!!

DON'T BE RECKLESS! I HAVEN'T HAD ANY EXERCISE FOR ALL THESE YEARS...
BY NOW, MY BODY'S GROWN INTO THE SHAPE OF THIS BOX!
I CAN'T GET OUT, AND IF YOU BREAK THE CHEST YOU'LL BREAK ME WITH IT.

BUT...
HOW DID YOU GET HERE IN THE FIRST PLACE?

READ THIS WAY

YOU SAID YOU WERE A PIRATE?
THAT'S RIGHT! SO FAR I ONLY HAVE A CREW OF THREE.

WELL, I USED TO BE A PIRATE, TOO!
REALLY?
IT WAS GREAT! RISKING MY LIFE IN THE PURSUIT OF TREASURE!
IT'S FUN, HUH?

YOU GOT A TREASURE MAP?
I'VE GOT A MAP OF THE GRAND LINE!

I'M GOING AFTER THE ONE PIECE!!
WHAT!? THE ONE PIECE?
YOU'RE NOT SERIOUSLY THINKING ABOUT ENTERING THE GRAND LINE!?

SO...
WHERE IS THIS GRAND LINE?
I DON'T KNOW. CAN YOU TELL ME WHERE IT IS, MR. SHRUB?

I CAN'T READ MAPS!
HAHAHAHAHA
YOU CAN'T!?
HOW CAN THEY CALL THEM-SELVES PIRATES?
PATHETIC...

OKAY, LOOK!
FWIP
YOU KNOW WHERE THE RED LINE IS, RIGHT?

YEAH...
IT'S THE STRIP OF LAND THAT DIVIDES THE OCEANS.

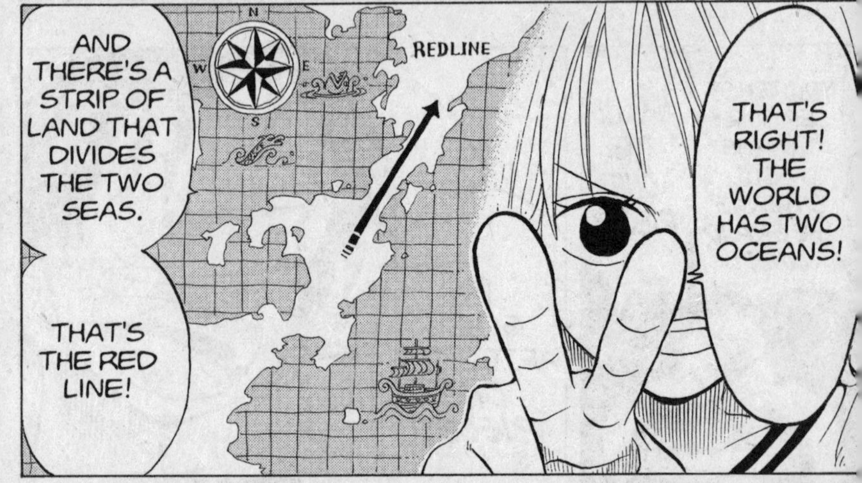
THAT'S RIGHT! THE WORLD HAS TWO OCEANS!
N
W
E
S
REDLINE
AND THERE'S A STRIP OF LAND THAT DIVIDES THE TWO SEAS.
THAT'S THE RED LINE!

NOW, THERE'S A TOWN AT THE CENTER OF THE RED LINE...

AND THERE'S A SEA ROUTE THAT CUTS THROUGH THAT TOWN AND GOES AROUND THE WORLD.

THAT'S THE GRAND LINE!!

GRAND LINE

REDLINE

GOLD ROGER, THE KING OF PIRATES, WAS THE ONLY PERSON WHO EVER MANAGED TO RULE IT.
THEY SAY IT'S THE MOST DANGEROUS SEA ROUTE.
IF THE ONE PIECE IS SOMEWHERE ALONG THAT LINE...
HMM. ALL WE HAVE TO DO IS SAIL AROUND THE WORLD!

DON'T BE DENSE! IT'S NOT SO EASY!
THEY ALSO CALL THE GRAND LINE THE PIRATES' GRAVEYARD, Y'KNOW!

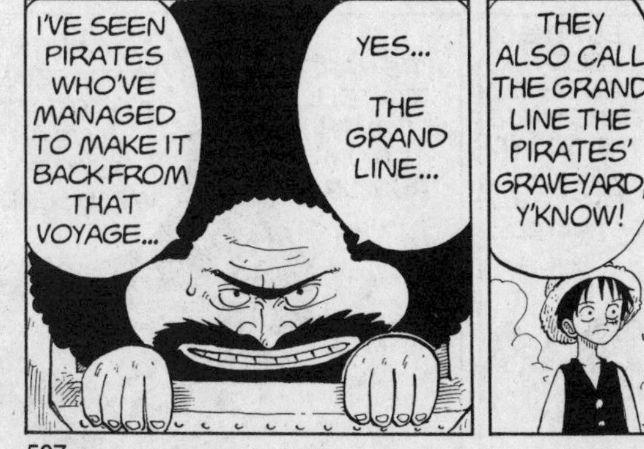
YES... THE GRAND LINE...
I'VE SEEN PIRATES WHO'VE MANAGED TO MAKE IT BACK FROM THAT VOYAGE...

READ THIS WAY

THEY'RE BROKEN MEN, ALMOST ZOMBIES!
YOU CAN TELL JUST BY LOOKING AT 'EM...
WHETHER PIRATES OR MONSTERS...
THEY'VE SEEN TERRIBLE THINGS.

NONE WILL SPEAK OF IT...
BUT THE SIGHT OF 'EM'S PROOF ENOUGH...
THE GRAND LINE IS A PLACE OF HORROR!
...!
ULP

TO FIND THE ONE PIECE AND COME BACK ALIVE IS ALMOST IMPOSSIBLE!
IT'S HARD TO TELL TRUTH FROM RUMOR...
BUT IT'S BEEN TWENTY-ODD YEARS SINCE THE GREAT AGE OF PIRATES STARTED...
AND NO ONE'S GOT THAT LEGENDARY TREASURE YET.

UNDERSTAND? THE SEARCH FOR THE ONE PIECE IS A FOOL'S DREAM!
MAYBE SO...
BUT I THINK WE'LL FIND IT.
GIVE IT UP! THERE'S PLENTY OF OTHER TREASURE TO BE HAD.
WHY GET OUR-SELVES KILLED?

WE'LL FIND IT! I'M VERY LUCKY!
FINE... I DON'T KNOW WHERE YOUR CONFI-DENCE COMES FROM...

I'LL TELL YOU WHY I HAVEN'T LEFT THIS ISLAND!
WHAT, MR. SHRUB MAN?

HOPE!
I STILL HAVE HOPE!

READ THIS WAY

ABOUT WHAT?

TWENTY YEARS AGO...
I WAS A PIRATE WHEN I CAME TO THIS ISLAND.
WE'D HEARD THERE WAS TREASURE HERE.

WE EVEN HAD A MAP OF IT.
IT'S NO USE SEARCHING THIS ISLAND ANYMORE!
ALL 200 OF US HAVE BEEN HUNTING FOR THREE WEEKS...
WACK!

AND ALL WE'VE FOUND IS ONE BROKEN, EMPTY TREASURE CHEST!

ALL HANDS BACK TO THE SHIP!!
YARR!!
HEY, GAIMON, COME ON!
WE'RE LEAVING!
ALL RIGHT!
GAIMON (20 YEARS AGO)

HMM, THAT CLIFF...
THE CAPTAIN WAS STANDING IN FRONT OF IT THE WHOLE TIME.
I WONDER IF ANYONE ACTUALLY WENT UP THERE AND LOOKED?
KRFF
...UNH...
...UNH...
WAP
KRFF
!!!
I COULDN'T BELIEVE MY EYES!
IT'S UP HERE!!!
TA-
DA
I FOUND IT!
HEY, EVERY-BODY!!
SLIP
!!?
GYAAAAAA!!!
FOOM
WUNK
AND I FELL INTO THIS TREASURE CHEST AND GOT STUCK!

WHEN I WOKE UP...
SHUFFLE
AAAA AAH!
TH- THEY'RE SAILING!!!
MY CREWMATES HAD ALREADY SET SAIL...
HMMM...
THAT MEANS THE TREASURE IS ALL MINE!
HOORAY!!!
TUMP
ARRGGGHH!!!
I CAN'T CLIMB UP THE CLIFF LIKE THIS! I'M STUCK!!
COME BACK, YOU GUYS!
AND NOBODY'S BEEN HERE FOR 20 YEARS?
NO, PEOPLE CAME...
LOTS OF PEO-PLE...
MOSTLY PIRATES LOOKING FOR TREASURE. BUT I SCARED 'EM ALL OFF WITH MY TRIAL OF THE FOREST BIT.

ALL THAT TREASURE I SAW UP ON THE CLIFF...
I JUST CAN'T BRING MYSELF TO PART WITH IT.

IF ONLY I WEREN'T STUCK IN THIS CHEST!
ALL THIS TIME, I'VE PROTECTED THAT TREASURE!
IT'S MINE! ALL MINE!!!

YOU'RE ABSOLUTELY RIGHT!

IT'S RIGHTFULLY YOURS!!

GAIMON! I'LL GO UP THERE AND GET THAT TREASURE FOR YOU!
REALLY? THAT WOULD BE GREAT!!
YE—AH!
I'M GLAD I TOLD YOU MY STORY!

BUT YOU'RE A PIRATE AND A THIEF.
SHUT UP! I'M A THIEF, BUT I'M NOT HEARTLESS!

DA—DOOM

HERE WE ARE!

THIS IS IT!

IT'S BEEN A WHILE SINCE I CAME HERE.

WHY DIDN'T YOU TELL ANYBODY ELSE YOUR STORY?

LIKE YOU TOLD US?

I NEVER TRUSTED ANYBODY.

NONE OF THE OTHERS EVER TRIED TO TALK TO ME.

BESIDES...

OH BOY!! THE TREASURE IS SO CLOSE!!!

FINALLY!!

TODAY'S THE DAY!!

READ
THIS
WAY

LUFFY...
DO YOUR STUFF.
YOU WANT *ME* TO DO IT?
WUP

WELL, I CERTAINLY CAN'T CLIMB THAT SHEER CLIFF!
I'M COUNTING ON YOU, STRAW HAT BOY!
OKAY...

BREEEN

WUK

WOW!!

SPROING!

HE DID IT!!

I SEE THEM!!!
FIVE TREASURE CHESTS!!!
YIPPEE!!
THROW 'EM DOWN HERE!
BUT DON'T DROP THEM ON US!
HA HA HA HA HA!

FORGET IT!

HUH!?
...
LUFFY, ARE YOU INSANE?
STOP JOKING AROUND AND THROW 'EM DOWN HERE!!

FORGET IT! I DON'T WANT TO!
DARN IT, LUFFY!
IT'S OKAY. HE DOESN'T WANT TO DO IT.
HOW CAN YOU SAY THAT? IT'S *YOUR* TREASURE!
STRAW HAT BOY!
Y-YOU'RE...
YOU'RE A GOOD KID!!!

WHAT!?
SNIF SNIF...
I SUSPECTED THIS MIGHT BE THE CASE...
I HAD MY FEARS...
...
BUT...
FWUMP
I JUST DIDN'T WANT TO BELIEVE IT.

THEY'RE EMPTY...

BOO

...AREN'T THEY?

WHAT?

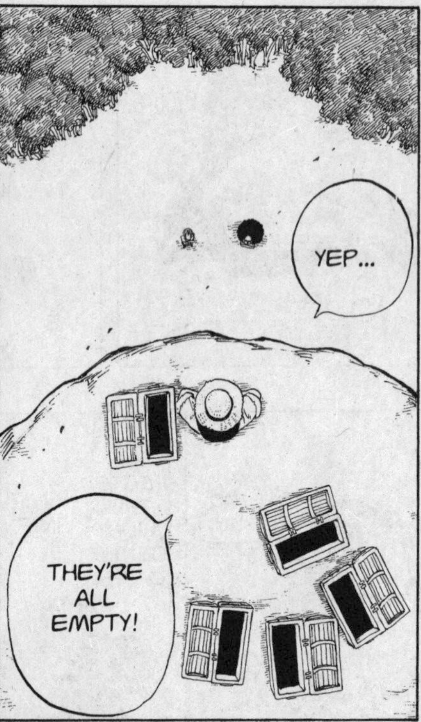
YEP...
THEY'RE ALL EMPTY!

IT HAPPENS ALL THE TIME...
WITH TREASURE MAPS...
SOB
YOU GET YOUR HANDS ON A TREASURE MAP, BUT SOME-ONE'S ALREADY TAKEN THE LOOT...

READ THIS WAY

BUT YOU'VE BEEN GUARDING THEM FOR 20 YEARS!
AND THEY WERE EMPTY...

...

HA HA HA HA HA HA HA HA!!
HA HA HA HA HA HA HA HA
DON'T FEEL BAD, MR. SHRUB HEAD!! YOU'RE LUCKY WE SHOWED UP!

ANOTHER 30 YEARS AND YOUR WHOLE LIFE WOULD HAVE PASSED YOU BY!
KID...

LUFFY...

WELL, ONLY ONE THING WILL MAKE UP FOR A DISAPPOINTMENT LIKE THIS...
YOU'RE GOING AFTER THE ONE PIECE WITH ME.

YOU WANT...
YOU WANT ME TO JOIN YOUR CREW?

ARE YOU SURE?
YOU REALLY WANT TO STAY ON THIS ISLAND?

SPWOOSH

YES...
NICE OF YOU TO ASK ME TO JOIN YOU, BUT THIS IS MY HOME!
THERE'S NO TREASURE, BUT I CAN STILL BE THE GUARDIAN OF THE FOREST!
WHY?

DID YOU SEE ALL THE UNUSUAL ANIMALS THAT LIVE IN THE FOREST?
ALL THOSE WEIRD SNAKE-RABBITS AND LION-PIGS?
MORE PEOPLE COME TO THIS ISLAND LOOKING FOR EXOTIC ANIMALS THAN FOR TREASURE.
I'VE GROWN FOND OF THOSE CRITTERS AFTER ALL THESE YEARS.
I DON'T WANT TO ABANDON THEM.

IN A WAY, I'M RELIEVED THAT THERE'S NO TREASURE.
I CAN FINALLY STOP FRETTING ABOUT IT AND ENJOY THIS ISLAND!
TOO BAD YOU WON'T BE COMING WITH US. I KINDA LIKE YOU.
YOU'RE SORT OF AN EXOTIC ANIMAL YOURSELF!
WATCH IT, BUSTER!!

YOU'LL GET YOURSELF A GREAT CREW!!
NOW GO FIND THE ONE PIECE...
AND MAKE THE WORLD YOUR OYSTER!!
THANKS! I WILL!
SEE YA!

AND SO LUFFY AND HIS FRIENDS LEAVE GAIMON ON HIS ISLAND...
AND RESUME THEIR VOYAGE TO THE GRAND LINE!

Coloring Page

NAVIGATION

Chapter 23:
THE DREAD CAPTAIN USOPP

READ THIS WAY

WE'RE BEING RASH...
DO-OM

WHY?
WE CAN'T SAIL THE ***GRAND LINE*** LIKE THIS!

YOU'RE RIGHT! THAT SHRUB MAN GAVE US A LOT OF FRUIT...
...BUT WE NEED MEAT TO KEEP OUR STRENGTH UP!
I'M NOT TALKING ABOUT ***FOOD!***

SHE'S RIGHT - WE DON'T HAVE A DROP OF GROG ABOARD.
I'M NOT TALKING ABOUT BOOZE EITHER!

WE'RE HEADED FOR THE *GRAND LINE*-- THE MOST DANGEROUS SEA LANE IN THE WORLD!
AND DON'T FORGET, THE MOST SUCCESSFUL PIRATES ALIVE ARE AFTER THE *ONE PIECE*, TOO!
AND THEIR SHIPS ARE BIG AND STURDY...

OURS ARE LITTLE TUBS, AND WE DON'T EVEN HAVE A CREW...
IF WE GO ON LIKE THIS, WE'LL NEVER SURVIVE THIS FOOLHARDY VENTURE.

SO WHAT SHOULD WE DO?
WE'RE GOING TO PLAN AHEAD AND PREPARE!
THERE'S A VILLAGE A LITTLE SOUTH OF HERE...

OUR FIRST PRIORITY IS TO ACQUIRE A PROPER VESSEL.
AND EAT MEAT!!

READ THIS WAY

AHH! A NEW DAY!

SKREE

PLOOSH

SKREE

THE SUN SHINES BRIGHT AND CHEERFUL ON THE SEA!

USOPP
VILLAGE YOUTH

TWEET

TWEET

HORRORS!
TMP TMP TMP
WE'RE DOOMED!
THE PIRATES ARE COMING!!
THEY'RE ATTACKING THE VILLAGE!!
WAAAAAAHH!
RUN FOR YOUR LIVES!!

WHAT PIRATES!?
PIRATES!!
WELL, THAT'S USOPP'S MORNING COMMOTION. I'D BEST BE OFF TO WORK...
THE PIRATES ARE COMING!!!
FWAP
HE'S AT IT AGAIN...

DA-DUM
JUST KIDDING!!!
HA HA HA HA HA HA HA HA!!

KLANK!
UNGH!

YOU LYING BRAT!
TODAY I'M GONNA TEACH YOU A LESSON!

KLAK
KLAK KLAK
OOH!
HERE THEY COME!!

READ
THIS
WAY

COME BACK HERE, LIAR!!!
TMPTMPTMP
WA HA HA HA! CATCH ME IF YOU CAN!!!

DARN! HE GOT AWAY AGAIN!
THAT YAHOO'S ALWAYS CAUSING TROUBLE!
I'LL TEACH HIM!

.....
KRESH...
WHERE'D HE GO?

HEE HEE HEE HEE HEE!
I FOOLED ALL THE VILLAGERS AGAIN!

READ THIS WAY

HAH! I DID IT AGAIN TODAY!
KRESH
JUST A LITTLE JOLT OF EXCITE-MENT TO ENLIVEN THIS BORING LITTLE VILLAGE!!

THERE HE IS!!
HUH?

HEY!
IT'S *YOU* GUYS!

TA—DA!

AYE, CAPTAIN USOPP!

GOOD MORNING, SIR!

YOUR PIRATE CREW REPORTING FOR DUTY!

PEPPER
VILLAGE BOY

CARROT
VILLAGE BOY

READ THIS WAY

PEPPER! CARROT! JUST THE TWO OF YOU?
WHERE'S ONION?

STILL SLEEPING, I GUESS.
RIGHT?
YEAH, PROBABLY...

THAT BOY...
WAAAAHHH!
!?

HORRORS!!
TMPTMPTMPTMP
HEY, IT'S ONION!
WHAT'S HE GOING ON ABOUT?

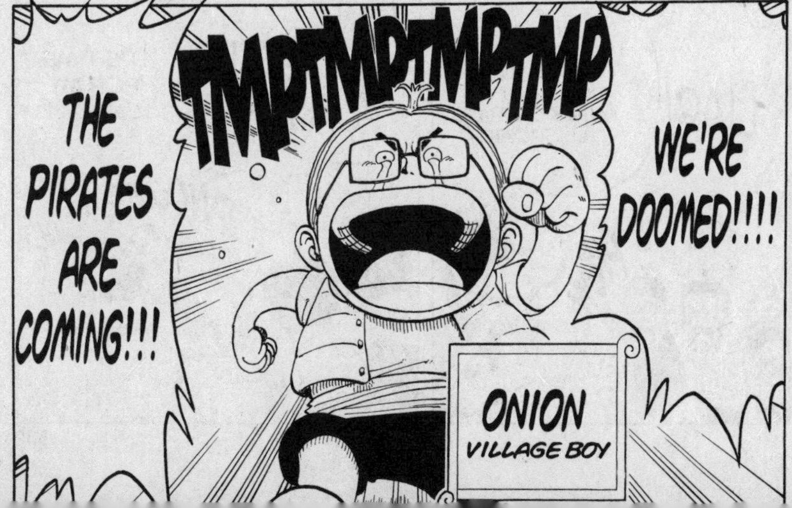
WE'RE DOOMED!!!!
TMPTMPTMPTMP
THE PIRATES ARE COMING!!!
ONION
VILLAGE BOY

A SHIP FLYING THE SKULL AND CROSS-BONES IS COMING FROM THE NORTH!!
IT'S TRUE! I SAW 'EM WITH MY OWN EYES!!

LIAR!
IT'S TRUE!!

FWOOM
ITS SAIL HAS THE SIGN OF BUGGY THE CLOWN!!

YOU'RE NOT LYING?
IT'S TRUE! WE'RE IN DANGER!!

IT'S TIME FOR MY SNACK!!
DON'T RUN AWAY!!
FWOOM

I HAVE A MEDICAL CONDITION--IF I DON'T EAT MY SNACK ON TIME, I'LL CROAK...
LIAR!
PHEW

READ THIS WAY

CAPTAIN, DON'T YOU WANT TO BECOME A REAL PIRATE!?
A REAL PIRATE WOULDN'T BE SCARED OF OTHER PIRATES!
YEAH! AND THERE'S ONLY THREE OF 'EM!

ONLY THREE?
THEN IT'S NOT A BIG SHIP?
NO, JUST TWO LITTLE ONES.

ALL RIGHT! USOPP'S PIRATE CREW, PREPARE FOR ACTION!
WE'LL DEFEND OUR VILLAGE!!

OKAY, LET'S GO! FOLLOW ME!!
.....
YAAAR!

UH...
OKAY!!

WHAT DO YOU KNOW? THERE REALLY IS AN ISLAND HERE!

OF COURSE THERE IS.

IT'S RIGHT HERE ON THE MAP.

TUMP

HMM...

AND THERE'S A VILLAGE HERE?

YEAH, BUT IT LOOKS PRETTY SMALL.

READ THIS WAY

HEY, ONION, IS THAT THEM? ARE THOSE THE PIRATES?
YEAH, THEIR SAIL HAD A SKULL ON IT!
THEY DON'T LOOK VERY SCARY TO ME...
YEAH.

...

AHHH! SOLID GROUND AT LAST!
WHAT? YOU SLEPT THE WHOLE WAY.

SO...
WHAT DO YOU THINK IS UP...

WITH *THOSE* GUYS?
GASP!!
!!!

HEY, YOU GUYS!
DON'T RUN AWAY!!
WOMP!
TMP TMP TMP TMP
AAAGH! THEY SEE US!!!

.....

I AM THE NOTORIOUS CAPTAIN USOPP!!!

DO-OM!!

FEARED PIRATE, AND RULER OF THIS VILLAGE!!!

I HAVE 80 MILLION MEN POISED TO STOP YOU.
DA-DUM
SO YOU'D BETTER THINK TWICE BEFORE YOU INVADE!

LIAR!
DARN! SHE SAW THROUGH ME!
WOMP
SEE? I KNEW IT!
DARN! I ADMITTED THAT I LIED!
WOMP
SHE'S A MASTER OF INTERROGATION!

HA HA HA HA HA!! YOU'RE FUNNY!!

HAHAHA HAHA

HEY! ARE YOU LAUGHING AT ME!?

I'M A PROUD MAN!

WHICH IS WHY THEY CALL ME "PROUD CAPTAIN USOPP"!

BLAB
THE VILLAGE RESTAURANT
REALLY? YOU'RE LOOKING FOR A CREW?
MESHI
BLAB

BLAB
CREWMEN AND A BIGGER SHIP?
THAT'S RIGHT!
BLAB
WOW! WHAT A GREAT ADVENTURE!
BLAB BLAB

WELL, YOU WON'T FIND ANY GALLEONS HERE IN TOWN...
BUT THERE IS A PLACE YOU CAN GO.
WHERE?
THAT HUGE MANSION THAT STANDS OUT LIKE A SORE THUMB!
THAT'S WHERE!

READ THIS WAY

THE OWNER OF THE MANSION...
IS A YOUNG GIRL...
AND SHE'S BEDRIDDEN.

HMM...
HOW DID SHE BECOME THE OWNER OF A MANSION?

MORE MEAT, PLEASE!
AND MORE GROG!!
ARE YOU GUYS LISTENING TO MY STORY?

ABOUT A YEAR AGO...
BOTH THE POOR GIRL'S PARENTS GOT SICK AND DIED.
THEY LEFT HER WITH A HUGE INHERITANCE, A MANSION, AND A DOZEN SERVANTS.

SHE'S RICH AND LIVES IN LUXURY...
BUT NOBODY'S MORE UN-FORTUNATE THAN HER.

...

FORGET IT!
!?
WAP

WE'RE NOT GONNA FIND A SHIP HERE.
LET'S GO FIND ANOTHER TOWN.

OKAY. I GUESS WE CAN SPARE THE TIME...
AND I GOT A BELLYFUL OF MEAT!
LET'S GRAB SOME SUPPLIES AND GO!

BY THE WAY...
YOU SAID YOU WERE LOOKING FOR CREWMEN...
THAT'S RIGHT.

READ THIS WAY

I'M YOUR MAN!
I'LL BE YOUR CAPTAIN!
TA
DA

NO THANKS!
DON'T YOU WANT TO THINK IT OVER!?
WOMP

KLAHADORE ...?
WUFF
WUFF

YES, MISTRESS KAYA?

I WANT TO SEE...
I WANT TO SEE USOPP...

CABAJI THE ACROBAT
ZOLO THE SWORDS-MAN
HACHI THE MESSENGER
MOHJI THE ANIMAL TRAINER

Chapter 24:
THE LIE REJECTER

TMP TMP TMP TMP

YEAH, I SAW 'EM...
THEY TOOK THE CAPTAIN IN HERE.

ONION, ARE YOU SURE THOSE PIRATES WENT IN HERE?
SHHH!!

WE GOTTA SAVE HIM!
BUT REAL PIRATES ARE SAVAGES! THEY'LL EAT US!
DUMMY! **PIRATES** DON'T EAT PEOPLE! **OGRESSES** DO! NOW BE BRAVE!
THIS WILL BE THE GREATEST BATTLE THAT USOPP'S PIRATES HAVE EVER FOUGHT!!

WHAM!!
USOPP'S PIRATES...
?
HUH?
...ARE HERE!!
TA-DA!

WHO ARE THEY?
HUH.
BEATS ME.

HEY! WHERE'S THE CAPTAIN?
COULD THEY HAVE FINISHED WITH HIM ALREADY?

HEY, YOU PIRATES!
SLURP
WHAT'D YOU DO WITH OUR CAPTAIN?
......
GIVE HIM BACK!

AHHH!
THAT MEAT WAS DELICIOUS!
KLINK
!!
M-MEAT!?
GASP!
THE CAPTAIN!
HE COULDN'T HAVE--!
HEE
...

IF YOU'RE LOOKING FOR YOUR CAPTAIN ...
WHAT!? WHAT DID YOU DO TO HIM!?
HE JUST...
DO——OM
...GOT GOBBLED UP!

GYAAAAAH! OGRESS!!!
WHY ARE YOU LOOKING AT ME!?
AGAH
...!!
IT'S NOT FUNNY!
HA HA HA HA HA HA!!
WHAM!

"TIME TO GO"?
THAT'S WHAT HE SAID. THEN HE LEFT.

IT WAS PROBABLY TIME FOR HIM TO GO TO THE MANSION.
THE MANSION WHERE THE SICK GIRL LIVES?
YEAH.
WHY WOULD HE GO THERE?

TO TELL LIES!
THAT'S NOT VERY NICE.
YES IT IS! IT'S **VERY** NICE!
RIGHT?
YEAH, IT'S GREAT!
HUH?

THE MANSION
YOU WISH TO SEE USOPP?
IMPOSSIBLE!
KLAHADORE THE BUTLER
WHY? I JUST WANT TO TALK WITH HIM.
MUST I EXPLAIN AGAIN?
IT'S NOT PROPER FOR A LADY TO ASSOCIATE WITH THE BIGGEST LIAR IN THIS VILLAGE.
HE'S A BAD INFLUENCE.

READ THIS WAY
PHOOEY!
KAYA
MISTRESS OF THE MANSION
THAT'S FINE. THINK OF ME AS YOU WILL...
BUT I MUST PROTECT YOU.
YOUR BODY IS WEAK.
USOPP'S NONSENSICAL STORIES ARE TOO MUCH STIMULUS FOR YOU.
BUT I LIKE THEM.
PLEASE UNDERSTAND. YOUR LATE PARENTS ENTRUSTED ME WITH YOUR WELFARE.
AND I ***WILL*** WATCH OVER YOU.
FWUP

THAT'S WHY I HIRED GUARDS...
...AND TAKE ALL MANNER OF PRE-CAUTIONS...
.....

ALL FOR YOUR BEST INTEREST!!
FWUP
FWUP

YES...
...I KNOW...

I'M GLAD YOU UNDER-STAND.
I'LL LEAVE YOUR MEDICINE HERE. SEE THAT YOU TAKE IT.

WHAM
...OKAY...

READ THIS WAY

TINKTINK
!
USOPP!
YOU'RE LOOKING AS UNHEALTHY AS EVER, MADAM!

I'M SORRY I CAN'T WELCOME YOU AS A PROPER GUEST.
KLAHADORE WON'T ALLOW IT.
HE'S NOT REALLY A BAD PERSON, THOUGH...
I DON'T CARE. I LIKE BEING OUT HERE ANYWAY. I WOULDN'T FEEL COMFORTABLE IN YOUR FANCY OLD MANSION.

AFTER ALL...
...I'M A BRAVE AND GALLANT PIRATE!

WHAT'S TODAY'S ADVENTURE?
WELL?
HUFF
HUFF

TODAY I'M GOING TO TELL YOU SOMETHING THAT HAPPENED WHEN I WAS FIVE YEARS OLD.
I FOUGHT A GIANT GOLDFISH THAT LIVED IN THE SOUTH SEAS.
A GOLD-FISH?

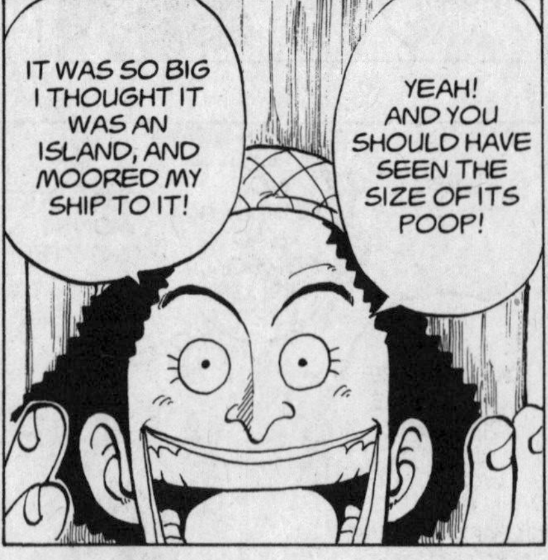
YEAH! AND YOU SHOULD HAVE SEEN THE SIZE OF ITS POOP!
IT WAS SO BIG I THOUGHT IT WAS AN ISLAND, AND MOORED MY SHIP TO IT!

HEY!
TA-DUM
HE IS A NICE GUY!

HE MAKES UP STORIES TO CHEER HER UP?
AND HE'S BEEN DOING IT FOR THE PAST YEAR?

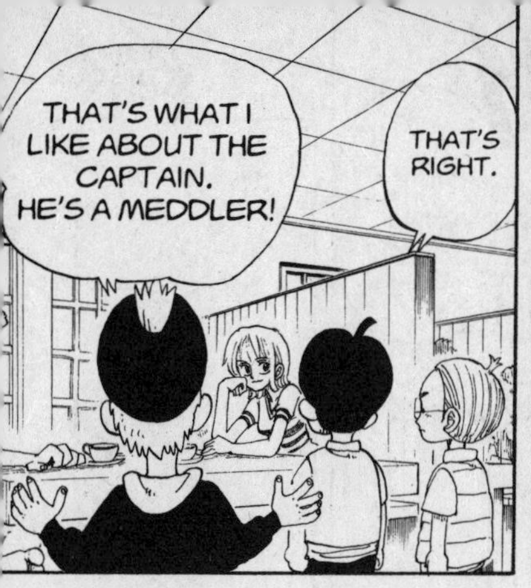
THAT'S RIGHT.
THAT'S WHAT I LIKE ABOUT THE CAPTAIN. HE'S A MEDDLER!

I LIKE THE CAPTAIN BECAUSE HE'S SO BOSSY!
I LIKE THE CAPTAIN BECAUSE HE'S SO BOASTFUL!
HMM... HE'S SURE GOT A LOT OF GOOD QUALITIES.

THEN THE GIRL'S SPIRITS MUST NOT BE TOO LOW.
THAT'S RIGHT! THANKS TO THE CAPTAIN!

DOOM
WELL, THAT SETTLES IT!!
LET'S GO ASK HER TO GIVE US A SHIP!

BUT WE ALREADY DECIDED AGAINST THAT IDEA!

READ THIS WAY

HEY, YOU!
TA—DOOM
GIVE US A SHIP!

OKAY, LET'S GO IN!
KLANK
CHINK
EVER HEAR OF KNOCKING?
THERE'S NO STOPPING HIM NOW.
FWUP
I GUESS WE'LL HAVE TO GO WITH HIM.

WHAT!?
INTRUDERS? WHERE ARE THE GUARDS?
THEY'RE ON THEIR LUNCH BREAK.

READ THIS WAY

HA HA HA! BUT WHAT DID YOU DO WITH THE GOLDFISH?
I CHOPPED IT UP AND TOOK IT TO A LAND OF LITTLE PEOPLE. THEY'RE STILL EATING IT TO THIS DAY.

AND AFTER SUCH A GLORIOUS FEAT, THE PEOPLE CALLED OUT TO ME--
CAPTAIN!!
THAT'S RIGHT! THEY CALLED ME--

GASP!
WHAT'RE *YOU* GUYS DOING HERE?
WE BROUGHT THESE GUYS WITH US!
FWIP
WHO ARE THEY?

YOU MUST BE THE MISTRESS OF THIS PLACE!

OH, THEY HEARD OF MY REPUTATION FROM AFAR, AND CAME TO SEEK ME OUT.
THEY'RE THE NEWEST MEMBERS OF MY CREW!
YEAH!
HEY! THAT'S NOT RIGHT!!

A FAVOR?
TO ASK OF ME?

YEAH!
WE WANT A BIG STURDY SHIP!
WHAT IS THE MEANING OF THIS!?

YOU REALIZE YOU'RE TRESPASSING?!
!
THE BUTLER!
KLAHA-DORE...
SHUF SHUF
WIP
WHAT'S HIS PROBLEM?

YOU SEE, THESE PEOPLE, THEY'RE--
SAVE YOUR EXCUSES FOR LATER.

YOU MUST ALL GO-- IMMEDIATELY.
OR DO YOU HAVE SOME BUSINESS HERE?

I WANT A BIG STURDY SHIP!
I CAN'T HELP YOU.

!
WAP

YOU...
YOU'RE USOPP, AREN'T YOU?
GASP

...!

YOUR REPUTATION PRECEDES YOU...
YOU'RE THE TALK OF THE VILLAGE.
UH... THANKS!
CALL ME "CAPTAIN USOPP," IF YOU PLEASE!
BUT REALLY, THERE'S NO NEED FOR FLATTERY!

THE GUARDS...
THEY'VE REPORTED SEEING YOU LURKING AROUND THE ESTATE.
DO YOU HAVE ANY BUSINESS BEING HERE?
FWUP

WELL...
YES. I DO.
I SAW A LEGENDARY *MOLE* ENTER THIS ESTATE. I'M TRYING TO CAPTURE HIM!

YOU'RE THE SON OF A FILTHY PIRATE.
I WOULDN'T PUT ANYTHING PAST YOU.
STAY AWAY FROM MISTRESS KAYA.

HMPH. YOU'VE A GIFT FOR DECEIT.
WHAT!?
I'VE ALSO HEARD STORIES OF YOUR FATHER.

...!
WOW! HIS FATHER'S A PIRATE?

...A FILTHY PIRATE...?

YOU AND MISTRESS KAYA ARE FROM COMPLETELY DIFFERENT WORLDS.
IS IT MONEY YOU'RE AFTER? HOW MUCH DO YOU WANT?
!

!

YOU'VE GONE TOO FAR, KLAHA-DORE!
YOU OWE USOPP AN APOLOGY!!
MISTRESS KAYA, WHY SHOULD I APOLOGIZE TO THIS TRASH?
I'M ONLY SPEAKING THE TRUTH!
BUT I DO FEEL SORRY FOR YOU...
YOUR TREASURE-CRAZED IDIOT FATHER DID ABANDON YOU.
KLAHA-DORE!!
STOP BAD-MOUTHING MY FATHER!!
WHAT ARE YOU GETTING SO WORKED UP ABOUT?
WHY NOT JUST FABRICATE SOME OF YOUR OUT-RAGEOUS LIES ABOUT YOUR FATHER?
JUST SAY HE'S REALLY A MERCHANT, OR THAT HE'S NOT YOUR REAL FATHER, OR PERHAPS...
...!!!

SHUT UP!!!
!!!!
!!
SEE HOW HE IS? HIS FIRST INSTINCT IS VIOLENCE!
HE'S AN ANIMAL-- LIKE HIS FATHER!
CAPTAIN!!
FWUP
SHUT UP!!

I'M PROUD THAT MY FATHER IS A PIRATE!!!
I'M PROUD THAT HE'S A BRAVE WARRIOR OF THE SEA!!!
YOU'RE RIGHT. I DO MAKE UP STORIES!
BUT THERE'S ONE THING I'LL NEVER LIE ABOUT!
I'LL NEVER LIE ABOUT MY PIRATE HERITAGE!!
...!!
I'M THE SON OF A PIRATE!!!
HEY, WAIT A MINUTE!
NOW I REMEMBER!

The Path To Becoming a Manga Character!

Part 2

Regarding the drawings on page 136:

This was the second draft of sketches I drew of Buggy's pirate crew. At this point I didn't make any changes to Buggy's appearance, so he's not included on this page.

Why is Zolo there?

In the early versions of the story, Zolo was a bodyguard on Buggy's ship before he joined Luffy. After a lot of thought, I decided not to do it that way.

Hachi the Messenger

Hachi the Messenger is a carrier pigeon. He relays messages between Buggy and his crew. He is an Opo bird, and his natural habitat appears to be the Grand Line.

Mohji Design Ideas

I found these sketches in my book of doodles, so I've included them here. They look pretty cool, too!

Chapter 25:
LIES

CAPTAIN...!

A PIRATE, A "BRAVE WARRIOR OF THE SEA"?
THAT'S A DECEITFUL WAY TO TWIST THE TRUTH.
FWUP
NONETHELESS, YOUR BEHAVIOR IS INDISPUTABLE PROOF OF YOUR RUFFIAN HERITAGE.

...!!

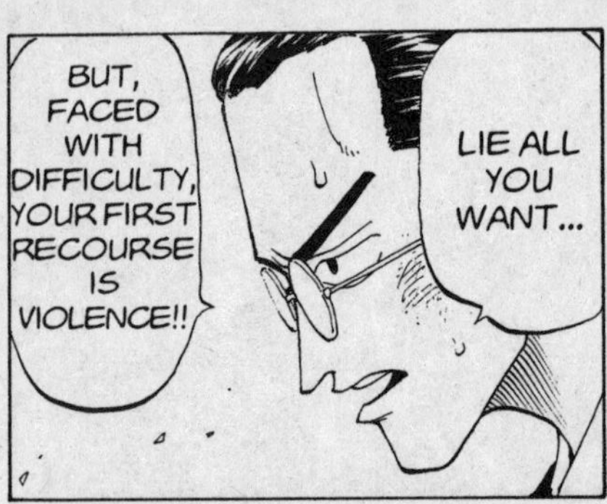
LIE ALL YOU WANT...
BUT, FACED WITH DIFFICULTY, YOUR FIRST RECOURSE IS VIOLENCE!!

I'M ONTO YOUR SCHEME, YOU SCALAWAG!
YOU'RE TRASH, LIKE YOUR PIRATE FATHER!!!

AND I KNOW YOU ARE ONLY KIND TO MISS KAYA BECAUSE YOU'RE AFTER HER.
WHAT!? I--

!!
THAT'S ENOUGH!!!
SWAP

STOP, USOPP!!!
PLEASE, NO MORE VIOLENCE!
!!

READ THIS WAY

....!!

KLAHA-DORE'S NOT A BAD PERSON...
HE TAKES CARE OF ME!

HE ONLY WANTS WHAT'S BEST FOR ME.
HE JUST... WENT TOO FAR...

...
LEAVE THE GROUNDS...

THIS IS NO PLACE FOR A RUFFIAN LIKE YOU!!
NEVER COME NEAR THIS ESTATE AGAIN!!
....!!

FINE, HAVE IT YOUR WAY...
I'M LEAVING.

AND I'M NEVER COMING BACK!
TMP TMP
CAPTAIN...

USOPP...

STUPID SMELLY *BUTT*-LER!! THE CAPTAIN'S A GREAT GUY!!
YEAH, FOOL!
DUMB-BELL!!

KNUCKLE-HEAD!!
YOU TOO, LUFFY?
BONK

.....!!
GYAAAA!!
C'MON AND FIGHT!
EASY, LUFFY!!
HMPH
AAAH

GET OFF THIS PROPERTY AT ONCE!!!

KOFF KOFF...
KNOCK KNOCK
KOFF KOFF

TIME FOR YOUR LUNCH, MISS KAYA...
KREEK
I DON'T WANT IT...
KOFF

I'M NOT HUNGRY.
IT'S NOT GOING TO TASTE GOOD.

YOU'LL UPSET THE COOK IF YOU SAY SUCH THINGS.
HE WORKS HARD TO CREATE HEALTHFUL, HEALING FOODS FOR YOU, MISS KAYA.
...

READ THIS WAY

MUST YOU MAKE ME FEEL GUILTY?
!

I FEEL BAD ENOUGH ABOUT GOING BEHIND YOUR BACK.
I TALKED TO USOPP AGAINST YOUR WISHES...
BUT YOU DIDN'T HAVE TO DRIVE HIM AWAY LIKE A DOG!

...

MAY I SIT?
YES.

FWUMP
...

THREE YEARS AGO...
...I CAME TO THIS ESTATE.
I'LL NEVER FORGET THAT DAY.

READ THIS WAY

BEFORE THAT, I HAD WORKED ABOARD A SHIP.
I MADE ONE SMALL MISTAKE, AND THEY MAROONED ME HERE.
I WAS FORSAKEN AND ALONE. FINALLY, I WANDERED INTO THIS VILLAGE.

I WAS PENNILESS, HOMELESS AND HELPLESS. I WOULD SURELY HAVE ENDED UP DEAD IN A DITCH.
THEN YOUR FATHER TOOK PITY ON ME.
I OWE MY LIFE TO YOUR LATE PARENTS!

AND YOU...
YOU ARE THE DAUGHTER OF MY BENE-FACTORS.
...
I REALIZE I WENT TOO FAR...
I'VE NO RIGHT TO INTERFERE WITH YOUR CHOICE OF FRIENDS.

READ THIS WAY

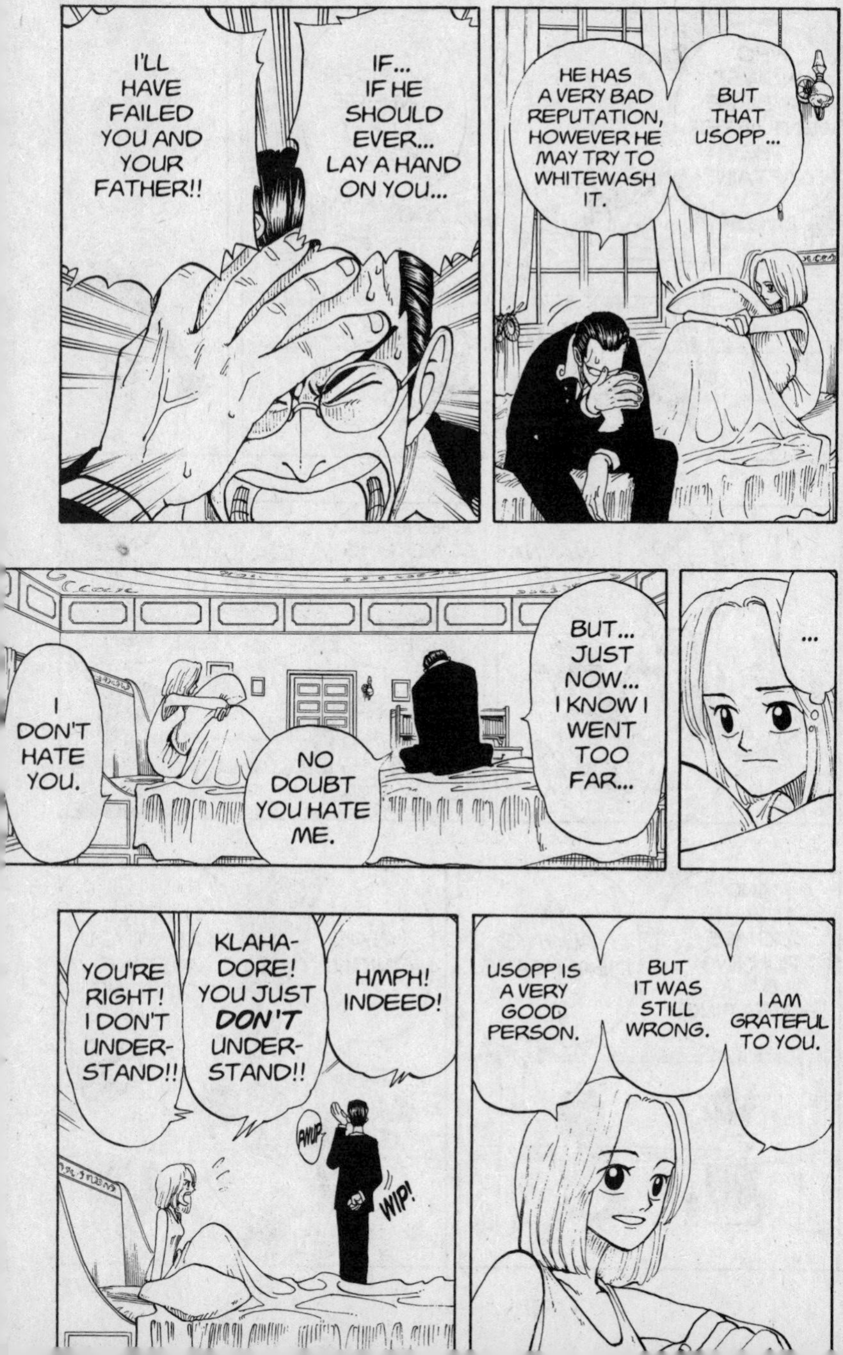

BUT THAT USOPP...
HE HAS A VERY BAD REPUTATION, HOWEVER HE MAY TRY TO WHITEWASH IT.
IF... IF HE SHOULD EVER... LAY A HAND ON YOU...
I'LL HAVE FAILED YOU AND YOUR FATHER!!

...
BUT... JUST NOW... I KNOW I WENT TOO FAR...
NO DOUBT YOU HATE ME.
I DON'T HATE YOU.

I AM GRATEFUL TO YOU.
BUT IT WAS STILL WRONG.
USOPP IS A VERY GOOD PERSON.
HMPH! INDEED!
KLAHA-DORE! YOU JUST **DON'T** UNDER-STAND!!
YOU'RE RIGHT! I DON'T UNDER-STAND!!
WIP!

I WONDER WHERE LUFFY WENT...
WHO KNOWS? MAYBE HE WENT AFTER THE "CAPTAIN."

WE KNOW WHERE THE CAPTAIN WENT!
YEAH! TO THE BEACH!
WHENEVER SOMETHING HAPPENS, THAT'S WHERE HE GOES!!
WANNA SEE?
NO THANKS...

HEY, AREN'T YOU MISSING SOMEONE?
YEAH, ONION!

HE ALWAYS DISAPPEARS...
AND THEN HE COMES RUNNING BACK SCREAMING.

WAAA-AHHH!!
IT'S HORRIBLE!! A BACKWARDS MAN!!
TMP TMP TMP
ONION!

TMPTMPTMP
IT'S HORRIBLE!!! WAAAH!!
A BACKWARDS MAN!!!

THERE'S A STRANGE MAN HEADED THIS WAY WALKING BACKWARDS.
LIAR!
IT'S TRUE!!!

LOOK!!

?

SHUF
SHUF...

SHUF
SHUF

READ THIS WAY
DA-DOOM
HEY! WHO JUST CALLED ME STRANGE?
I'M NOT STRANGE!!!
YOU'RE A LITTLE STRANGE.
DON'T BE SILLY. I'M JUST YOUR TYPICAL TRAVELING HYPNOTIST.
WOW! A HYPNO-TIST!
SHOW US A TRICK!
YEAH! SHOW US!
WHAT?
DJANGO THE HYPNOTIST
SHUF

OH, WELL... LOOK AT THE RING...
THEN YOU ARE GONNA PERFORM?

DON'T BE SILLY. I DON'T EVEN KNOW YOU.
WHY SHOULD I PERFORM FOR SOMEONE I'VE ONLY JUST MET?

WHEN I SAY, "ONE, TWO, DJANGO," YOU'LL FALL SOUND ASLEEP.
READY? ONE...
TW--

TWO...
...

DJANGO!
FWUMP
ZZZ
WUMP
WUMP
WUMP...
NOW THAT'S STRANGE!!!

READ THIS WAY

KRSSH

PLOOSH

HEY!
HERE YOU ARE!
DOINK!!
GASP

TA—DAH
DON'T SNEAK UP LIKE THAT!

YASOPP.
HE'S YOUR FATHER, RIGHT?
!
TUMP

...!!
HUH...?

READ
THIS
WAY

HOW DO YOU KNOW MY FATHER'S NAME?
WUNK

I MET HIM WHEN I WAS A KID.
WHAT!? REALLY!? YOU MET MY FATHER?
YUP!

I THOUGHT YOU LOOKED FAMILIAR WHEN I SAW YOU.
AND YOU LOOK JUST LIKE HIM.
I JUST FIGURED OUT WHY.
...

DO YOU KNOW WHERE MY FATHER IS NOW!?
NOPE!

YASOPP IS A CREWMAN ON MY FAVORITE PIRATE SHIP!
BUT I'M SURE HE'S STILL WITH CAP'N "RED-HAIRED" SHANKS!!

REALLY? HUH?

READ THIS WAY

SO HE'S WITH CAPTAIN SHANKS...
..."RED-HAIRED" SHANKS, EH?
KRSSH

HE'S WITH SHANKS!?
YOU'VE HEARD OF SHANKS?
!
ULP!!
BLOINK

OF COURSE I HAVE. HE'S A GREAT PIRATE!!
MY FATHER'S WITH A FAMOUS PIRATE CREW?

SPEAKING OF GREAT, I RECALL YASOPP WAS A GREAT SHOT.
I NEVER SAW HIM MISS.

BAM!!
WOW! YOU'RE AMAZING!
YASOPP
AW, THAT'S NOTHIN'. I CAN SHOOT THE WHISKERS OFF AN ANT AT 50 PACES!

GLUG!
Y'KNOW, LUFFY, I GOT A SON...
WHAM!
HE'D BE JUST ABOUT YOUR AGE!
WAP
NOT AGAIN! YOU'VE TOLD ME THIS A THOUSAND TIMES!
YASOPP

AND YOU'RE GONNA HEAR ABOUT HIM A THOUSAND TIMES MORE!!
GYAA!!
BONK
WOINKWOINK
IT'S A HARD THING TO BE PARTED FROM MY SON.
BUT I HAD NO CHOICE!
THAT PIRATE FLAG KEPT CALLING ME!!
YEAH-

YASOPP WAS A GREAT PIRATE!
...

A GREAT PIRATE!

YESSIR! HE SAILED OFF INTO THE BOUNDLESS SEA.
MY FATHER'S OUT THERE RISKING LIFE AND LIMB, AND I'M PROUD OF HIM.
THAT BUTLER SAID SOME OBNOXIOUS THINGS ABOUT HIM!
HE'LL RUIN MY FATHER'S GOOD NAME.

SO... YOU'RE NEVER GOING BACK TO KAYA'S?
I DON'T KNOW... IF THAT BUTLER BEGS ME TO COME BACK...
THEN MAYBE I'LL GO SEE HER...

YEAH!!
I DON'T LIKE THAT GUY, EITHER!!

YOU MEAN THAT BUTLER?
YEAH, THAT BUTLER...
HEY! WHAT'S THAT BUTLER DOING HERE!?
GOING

THERE'S SOMEONE WITH HIM. A WEIRD GUY.
I'VE NEVER SEEN HIM BEFORE.

DJANGO, I INSTRUCTED YOU TO KEEP A LOW PROFILE.
WHAT WERE YOU DOING SLEEPING IN THE MIDDLE OF THE VILLAGE?
...
DON'T BE SILLY. I'M NOT STANDING OUT. IT'S NOT STRANGE AT ALL.

HAVE YOU PREPARED EVERYTHING NECESSARY TO CARRY OUT THE PLAN?

OF COURSE I HAVE.
OPERATION "MURDER MISS KAYA" IS READY TO GO ANY TIME.

!
MURDER MISS KAYA!?

One Piece Storyboards #8

さーて
ペロッ
これで身軽に
他人の刀は
大切に扱うもんだぜ!!
ゾロ
お!!?

Chapter 26:

CAPTAIN KURO'S PLAN

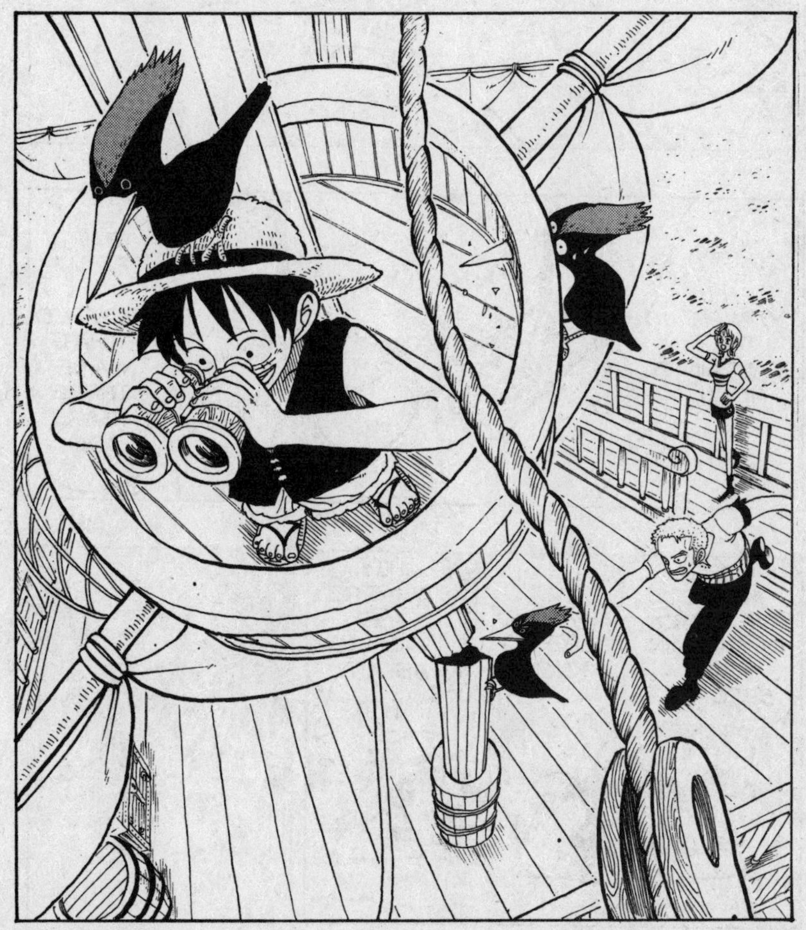

DJANGO, DJANGO. DON'T SAY "MURDER." IT SOUNDS SO SINISTER.

OH, YEAH. "ACCIDENT." IT'S GOING TO BE AN "ACCIDENT," RIGHT...

...CAPTAIN KURO?

QUIET, FOOL! I DISCARDED THAT NAME THREE YEARS AGO.
DON'T EVER CALL ME THAT.
YOU'RE THE CAPTAIN NOW.

...

HEY, WHAT'RE THEY TALKING ABOUT?
THAT'S WHAT I'D LIKE TO KNOW.
WAIT A MINUTE! I'VE HEARD OF CAPTAIN KURO BEFORE...

READ THIS WAY

HE WAS FAMOUS FOR HIS CAREFULLY-- PLANNED PILLAGING RAIDS.
BUT RUMOR WAS THAT THREE YEARS AGO, HE GOT CAUGHT BY THE NAVY AND EXECUTED.

TO TELL YOU THE TRUTH...
I WASN'T TOO SURE ABOUT THIS PLAN.

OH, NO?
IT WAS CRAZY. ALL OF A SUDDEN, YOU QUIT PIRATING.
YOU TAUGHT US ALL TO WORK WITHOUT YOU...

AND WE HELPED SPREAD THE RUMOR THAT YOU'D BEEN EXECUTED.
YOU CAME TO THIS VILLAGE...
NOW WE'RE BACK, THREE YEARS LATER, JUST LIKE YOU ORDERED.

READ
THIS
WAY

YOU'VE NEVER STEERED US WRONG BEFORE...
SO I'VE OBEYED YOUR ORDERS.
BUT MY SHARE OF THE SPOILS HAD BETTER BE WORTH IT.

YES...
IF MY PLAN SUC-CEEDS, YOU'LL GET WHAT YOU DESERVE.

DA-DUM
IF IT'S MURDER, THEN I'M YOUR MAN!

REMEMBER, YOU CAN'T JUST SLIT MISS KAYA'S THROAT, OR ANYTHING THAT CRUDE.
HER DEATH MUST APPEAR TO HAVE BEEN AN UNFOR-TUNATE ACCIDENT. DON'T FORGET IT.

IT APPEARS YOU STILL DON'T FULLY GRASP MY PLAN.
DON'T BE SILLY. I UNDER-STAND PERFECTLY.
WE WAIT FOR YOUR SIGNAL, THEN WE ATTACK THE VILLAGE.
WE KILL--UH, WE *ACCIDENT* THE GIRL TO DEATH...
AND YOU INHERIT HER FORTUNE.

FOOL! USE YOUR BRAIN!
HOW AM I GOING TO INHERIT HER FORTUNE?
KRAK
YOU JUST HAVE TO SERVE HER...
LISTEN, IDIOT. THIS IS THE CRUCIAL PART OF THE PLAN.

BEFORE YOU KILL HER, YOU HYPNOTIZE HER!
AND YOU MAKE HER WRITE A WILL THAT SAYS...
SHE LEAVES HER ENTIRE FORTUNE TO HER FAITHFUL BUTLER, KLAHADORE!
!

I'VE SPENT THE LAST THREE YEARS EARNING THE TRUST OF EVERYONE AROUND HER.
NO ONE WOULD QUESTION IT IF SHE LEFT EVERYTHING TO ME. I'VE EARNED IT.
THAT'S HOW I WILL INHERIT HER VAST FORTUNE!
VERY NATURALLY.

SO THAT'S WHY YOU WORKED AS A BUTLER FOR THREE YEARS.
WOULDN'T IT HAVE BEEN EASIER TO JUST BUST IN AND TAKE IT ALL AT GUNPOINT?
THAT'S THE CRUDE THINKING OF A PIRATE. YOU GET THE MONEY, BUT YOU HAVE TO LIVE LIKE A FUGITIVE.

WHAT GOOD ARE RICHES IF YOU'VE ALWAYS GOT THE NAVY CHASING YOU?
I'VE GONE LEGITIMATE. I'M A PACIFIST NOW.

READ
THIS
WAY

HAR HAR HAR! I GUESS THERE'S ALL KINDS OF PACIFISTS!
AND AFTER YOU WENT AND SLAUGHTERED THE GIRL'S WHOLE FAMILY!

I NEVER SLAUGHTERED ANYONE! KAYA'S PARENTS' DEATHS...
WELL, THAT WASN'T PART OF MY PLAN.

SURE, WHATEVER YOU SAY.
JUST HURRY UP AND GIVE US THE SIGNAL.
WE'VE BEEN ANCHORED OFFSHORE...
...FOR A WEEK NOW.

THOSE CUTTHROATS ARE READY TO CUT EACH OTHER'S THROATS BY NOW.
HEH HEH HEH HEH HEH HEH

....

WHAT DID THEY SAY? IT SOUNDED KINDA... MEAN.
WEREN'T YOU LISTENING!?
IT'S HORRIBLE! THEY'RE SERIOUS!

...
HOW HORRIBLE!! I'VE ***REALLY*** JUST HEARD SOMETHING HORRIBLE!!!
BA-BUMP
BA-BUMP
BA-BUMP

HE WAS AFTER KAYA'S FAMILY FORTUNE THIS WHOLE TIME!
FOR THREE YEARS HE'S BEEN PLOTTING TO GET IT ALL!
THAT BUTLER IS CAPTAIN KURO! HE'S STILL ALIVE!!

I PICKED THE WRONG GUY TO PUNCH OUT! HE'S GONNA KILL ME!!

THEY 'RE GONNA ATTACK THE VILLAGE AND KILL KAYA!!!
THIS IS HORRIBLE! REALLY HORRIBLE!
BA-BUMP
BA-BUMP

...
DON'T STAND UP! THEY'LL SEE YOU!
WUP

HEY! YOU GUYS!!

BA-BOOM!!

DON'T KILL KAYA!!!

!!?

!!!

WHO'S THAT!?

....!!

READ
THIS
WAY

YOU IDIOT! NOW THEY'VE SEEN US!!
KRK KRK
WE GOTTA RUN AWAY AND HIDE! THEY'LL MURDER US!!!

...
GRRR
WELL, WELL... IF IT ISN'T USOPP...

GASP
WAAAH!!
NOW, THEY'VE SEEN ME, TOO!!!

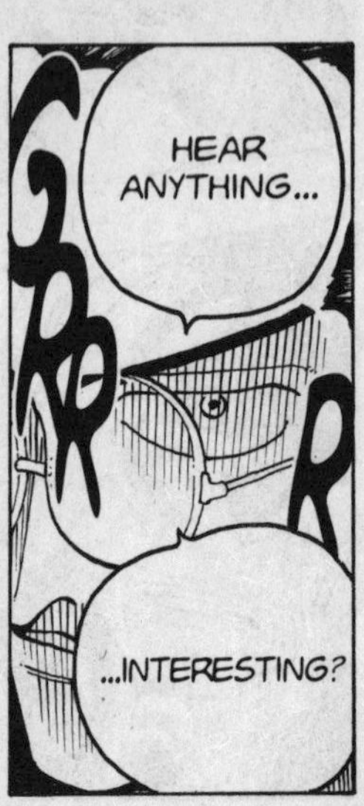
HEAR ANYTHING...
...INTERESTING?

NO-- I MEAN-- HUH!? I J-JUST GOT HERE, SO I COULDN'T HAVE--

WE HEARD EVERY-THING!
B-B-BUH-
TA-DAH!
SWAP

READ THIS WAY

...
...!
SO THEY HEARD US...

ALL RIGHT, THEN. YOU GUYS...
LOOK AT THIS RING.
NSH

WHAT'S THAT?
VEEN
OH NO! IT'S A WEAPON! HE'S GONNA KILL US!!

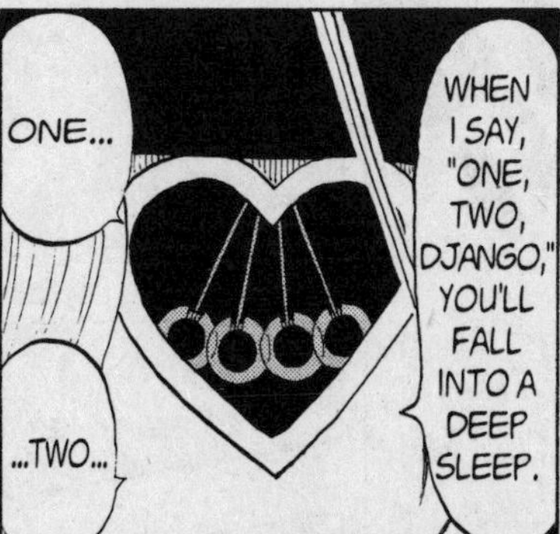
WHEN I SAY, "ONE, TWO, DJANGO," YOU'LL FALL INTO A DEEP SLEEP.
ONE...
...TWO...

TAKE COVER! HE'S GONNA GET US!
WUMP
...

DJANGO!

READ THIS WAY

ZZZZZZ
WUMP
?!

ZZZZZZ
BLAST IT, DJANGO, I THOUGHT YOU HAD THIS PERFECTED!

WUP

KRASH!!
!

HUH ?!
WHAT'RE YOU DOING!?
YOU'RE GONNA FALL!!!
SHF

!!!

READ THIS WAY

HEY!!!
YOU OKAY!?
WOOOO

HMM... DIDN'T MEAN TO KILL HIM.
HE FELL RIGHT ON HIS HEAD. FROM THAT HEIGHT, HE'S DEAD FOR SURE.
WAP

HE-- IT CAN'T BE--
HE KILLED HIM!!! KILLED HIM!!

WHAT SHOULD WE DO WITH THE OTHER ONE? KILL HIM, TOO?

THAT WON'T BE NECES-SARY.

NO ONE WILL BELIEVE ANYTHING THAT BUFFOON SAYS.

!?

!
DJANGO? TOMORROW, AT DAWN...
ATTACK THE VILLAGE.
CREATE A DISTRACTION, ROUGH UP SOME VILLAGERS...
AND KILL MISS KAYA.
...!!
TO-MORROW...

IT'S AS I SAID, USOPP.
NO ONE WILL BELIEVE WHAT YOU SAY, SO YOU CAN'T STOP ME!

...!!
CURSES! CURSES!

WHOOSH!!
WAAAAH!!!

YOU SURE IT'S OKAY?
OF COURSE. MY PLAN CAN'T FAIL.
SNORK
SNORK

PIRATES! PIRATES!
IT'S HORRIBLE!
TMP TMP TMP

TMP TMP TMP
THEY'LL ALL BE KILLED! EVERYONE IN THE VILLAGE I GREW UP IN!
THEY'LL KILL KAYA!
EVERYONE I LOVE!!

TMP TMP TMP
I LOVE THIS VILLAGE!!

WHO ARE YOU?
I'M USOPP, BRAVE WARRIOR OF THE SEA!

I HEARD YOU WEREN'T FEELING TOO WELL.
I'M HERE TO TELL YOU SOME STORIES TO CHEER YOU UP!

IT'S NONE OF YOUR BUSINESS! PLEASE LEAVE!
OR I'LL HAVE SOME-ONE SHOW YOU OUT!

TMP TMP TMP
...!

I WON'T HURT YOU!
I'M JUST A BUSY-BODY!

READ THIS WAY

WOAH... WHAT WAS THAT?
TMP TMP TMP TMP

WHOOSH !!
CAPTAIN!
HMM. I THOUGHT LUFFY WOULD BE WITH HIM.

IS HE STILL UPSET ABOUT WHAT THE BUTLER SAID ABOUT HIS FATHER?
WHO KNOWS...

NO! DID YOU SEE HIS FACE?
SOME-THING MUST'VE HAPPENED AT THE BEACH!!
HE WAS PALE AS A SHEET!!

...!!
HEY, HOW DO I GET TO THE BEACH?

I SMELL TROUBLE!
THAT HYPNOTIST WAS HEADED THAT WAY, TOO!
IT'S TIME FOR USOPP'S PIRATES TO TAKE ACTION!
YEAH, SURE, BUT SHOW ME THE WAY TO THE BEACH.

IT'S HORRIBLE!!
TMP TMP TMP TMP
EVERY BODY! LISTEN UP!
PIRATES ARE GONNA ATTACK US!!!

TOMORROW MORNING, PIRATES ARE GONNA ATTACK THIS VILLAGE!!!
HEAD FOR THE HILLS!!!

THAT LYING BRAT IS AT IT AGAIN!
THAT'S TWICE TODAY.
FORGET IT. JUST IGNORE HIS FOOL TALES.
AGAIN!? DURING LUNCH?
HE'S REALLY OVER-DOING IT LATELY...

THAT'S ENOUGH, USOPP!!
GRRR
GRRR
THAT'S ENOUGH FOR TODAY! NO MORE!!
NO! THIS TIME IT'S FOR REAL!!!

THAT'S WHAT YOU ALWAYS SAY!!
MAYBE IT'S TIME TO TEACH YOU A LESSON.

I'M ALWAYS JOKING AROUND...
BUT THIS TIME IT'S TRUE! YOU HAVE TO BELIEVE ME!
IF YOU WERE SERIOUS AND RESPONSIBLE LIKE MR. KLAHADORE, WE'D BELIEVE YOU...

IT DOESN'T MATTER WHAT YOU KNOW. YOU CAN'T INTERFERE WITH MY PLAN!

...!
BLAST IT!!

YOU GOTTA BELIEVE ME!! WE HAVE TO ESCAPE!
EVERYONE'S REALLY GONNA BE KILLED!!

FWAP
FWAP

THANK YOU, MY SEA-WOLVES, FOR COMING. IT'S BEEN THREE LONG YEARS.
IF THIS PLAN SUCCEEDS, YOU'LL ALL GET MORE THAN YOUR FAIR SHARE.
FWUP

TOMORROW AT DAWN! DESTROY THE VILLAGE!!!

HOORAY!!
AARRG!!
THREE CHEERS FOR CAPTAIN KURO!!

HAVE YOU SEEN KLAHA-DORE?
HE SAID HE HAD BUSI-NESS IN TOWN.
I SEE.

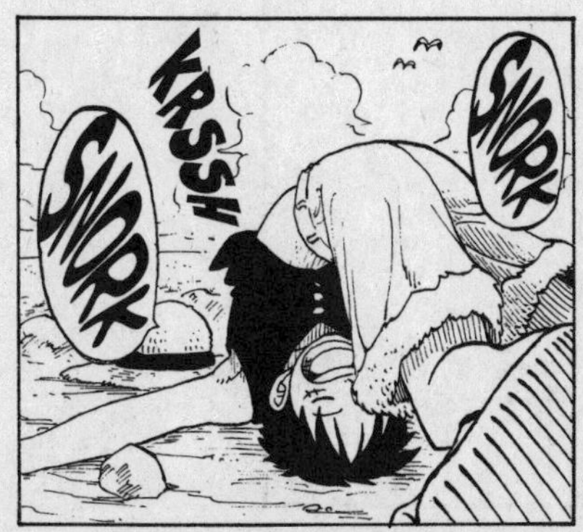
SNORK
KRSSH
SNORK

TO BE CONTINUED IN *ONE PIECE* VOL. 4!

Let's Make a Treasure Theater!

Behold! Treasure!
THE KING OF PIRATES
ONE PIECE

Part 1

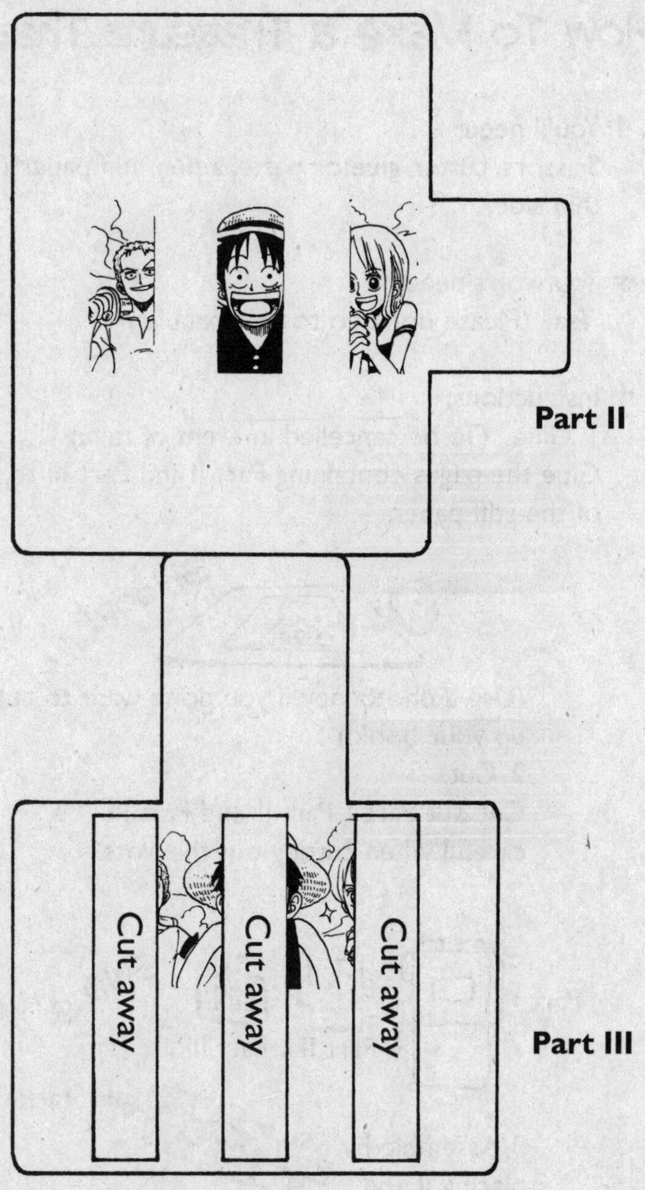
Part II
Cut away
Cut away
Cut away
Part III

See next page for assembly instructions!!

How To Make a Treasure Theater

✤ You'll need:
Scissors, cutter, glue or paste, a pen, stiff paper (on the thin side)

✤ You won't need:
Tea. (Please don't go to the trouble.)

✤ Instructions:
1. Glue. (To be cancelled in event of rain.)
Glue the pages containing Part II and Part III to a piece of the stiff paper.

Shloop!

(Use a photocopy if you don't want to cut up your book.)

2. Cut.
Cut out Part I, Part II, and Part III. Be careful when cutting out the slots.

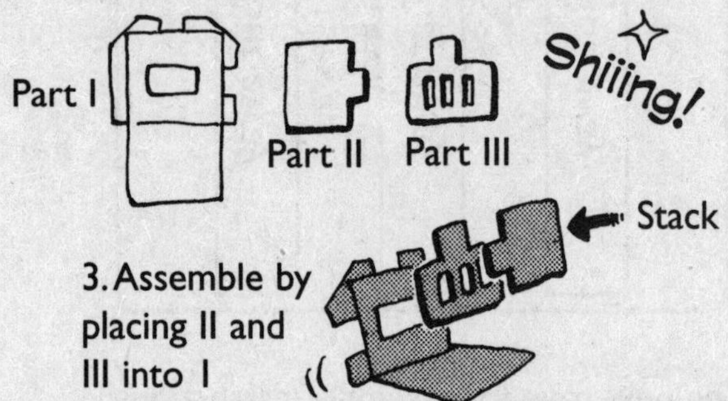
Part I
Part II
Part III
Shiiing!
Stack

3. Assemble by placing II and III into I

4. More glue.
Fold over Part I and apply glue.

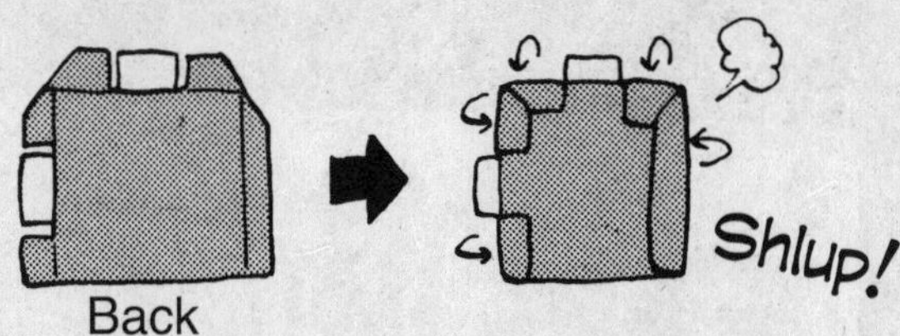
Back
Shlup!

5. Draw in the “Treasure.”

Ta-Daa!

When you pull the tab…a white surface appears! Draw in the picture or words that you'd like, and your Treasure Theater is complete!!
(It'll be even nicer if you color it.)

L.A. Corner!! (Little Apology)

I'm sorry. About what? About the Q&A Corner that I promised would be in this volume. Due to the production timeline of the comics, it couldn't be done. Will you forgive me if I say it'll be in the next volume? Aw, don't get mad. Don't cry. Don't hit me. I'll do it. Really, I will. Just wait for volume 4!

OMING NEXT VOLU

EAST BLUE
ONE PIECE
story and art by
Eiichiro Oda
Volume 4
Volume 5
Volume 6
ONE PIECE
story and art by
Eiichiro Oda
Volumes 4-5-6

Black Cat Pirates have landed… but if they want the village,
'll have to go through Luffy and his crew! How will Usopp's
shot, Zolo's swords, Nami's cunning, and Luffy's elastic punch
against the twisted mind and razor sharp claws of Captain K

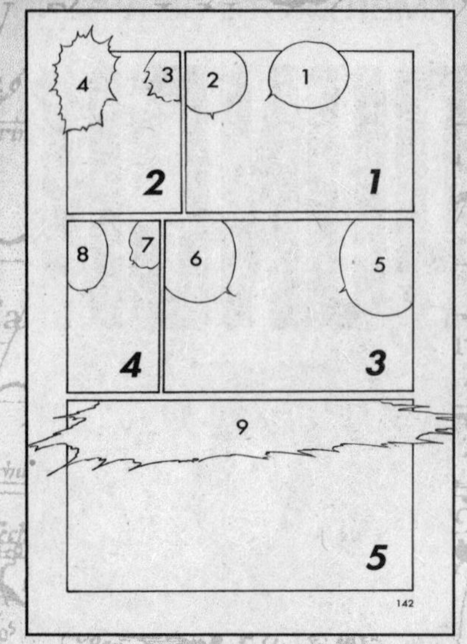
1
2
3
4
1
2
5
6
7
8
3
4
9
5
142

FOLLOW THE ACTION THIS WAY.

THIS IS THE LAST PAGE!

One Piece has been printed in the original Japanese format in order to preserve the orientation of the original artwork.

Please turn it around and begin reading from right to left. Unlike English, Japanese is read right to left, so Japanese comics are read in reverse order from the way English comics are typically read. Have fun with it!